MW00795381

Praise for *Nothing But You, Lord*

"Bishop Robert Barron and Fr. John Cush follow in the line of Irenaeus, Augustine, Basil, Ambrose, and so many others to this day: they are fine theologians precisely because they are fine pastors and formators. In *Nothing But You, Lord*, Fr. Cush offers us a timely and insightful synthesis of Bishop Barron's theology and spirituality of the Catholic priesthood and the pastoral and formational artistry involved in forming twenty-first-century priests."

—**Bishop John O. Barres**, Diocese of Rockville Centre,
from the foreword

"The priesthood is one of the most beautiful and challenging of vocations. It invites a man to conformity to Christ, to instrumental participation in Christ's sacramental economy, and to a responsibility for the mission of the Church in teaching and governance. Fr. John Cush in this work takes inspiration from the theology of Bishop Robert Barron, so as to present us with a spiritually balanced and theologically demanding vision of the priesthood and of seminary formation. An excellent reference for formators and seminarians, this work reflects both hope and experience. It is a sign of confidence in a constructive future for the Catholic priesthood, one founded upon truth and the desire for holiness."

—**Thomas Joseph White, OP**, Rector of the Pontifical University of
St. Thomas Aquinas, Rome

"When I first began teaching seminarians, I published a paper in the now defunct journal *Church*. When I went to look for my essay, another essay in the same issue caught my eye. It was Robert Barron's 'Priest As Doctor of the Soul.' It was a joyous read. There really was someone out there who looked upon priestly formation in mystical terms, refusing to reduce it to the popular emphasis at that time: professionalism. Here was a theologian who wanted to form priests in divine mystery so that they in turn could invite parishioners into the same. That was a vocation worth living. Now, in this book, we have Fr. John Cush's own mature thought on priestly formation woven together with Bishop Barron's image of priesthood and the thinking of the Church. All three strands knit a compelling read. I would hope that this book's vision of priesthood becomes a source for formators' imaginations. Every seminarian should read this work. It is a powerful gift to seminary formation."

—**Deacon James Keating**, Professor of Spiritual Theology, Kenrick-Glennon Seminary

"Fr. John Cush, a systematic theologian with long experience in seminary formation, offers a fine study and exposition of Bishop Barron's illuminating insights into priestly identity and formation. But Fr. Cush also speaks from his personal experience of the joys and challenges of priesthood. His book appears at a propitious time when the Church once again ponders the indispensable ministry of the priest, as it seeks to understand more fully, in synodal conversation, the meaning and implications of communion and mission in Christ."

—**Fr. Robert P. Imbelli**, priest of the Archdiocese of New York, author of *Christ Brings All Newness*

NOTHING BUT YOU, LORD

NOTHING BUT YOU, LORD

Reflections on the Priesthood and Priestly Formation through the Lens of Bishop Robert Barron

FR. JOHN P. CUSH

FOREWORD BY BISHOP JOHN O. BARRES

Published by Word on Fire, Elk Grove Village, IL 60007

Printed in the United States of America

Cover design by Cassie Bielak, typesetting by Marlene Burrell,
and interior art direction by Nicolas Fredrickson

ISBN: 978-1-68578-103-3

Library of Congress Control Number: 2023946602

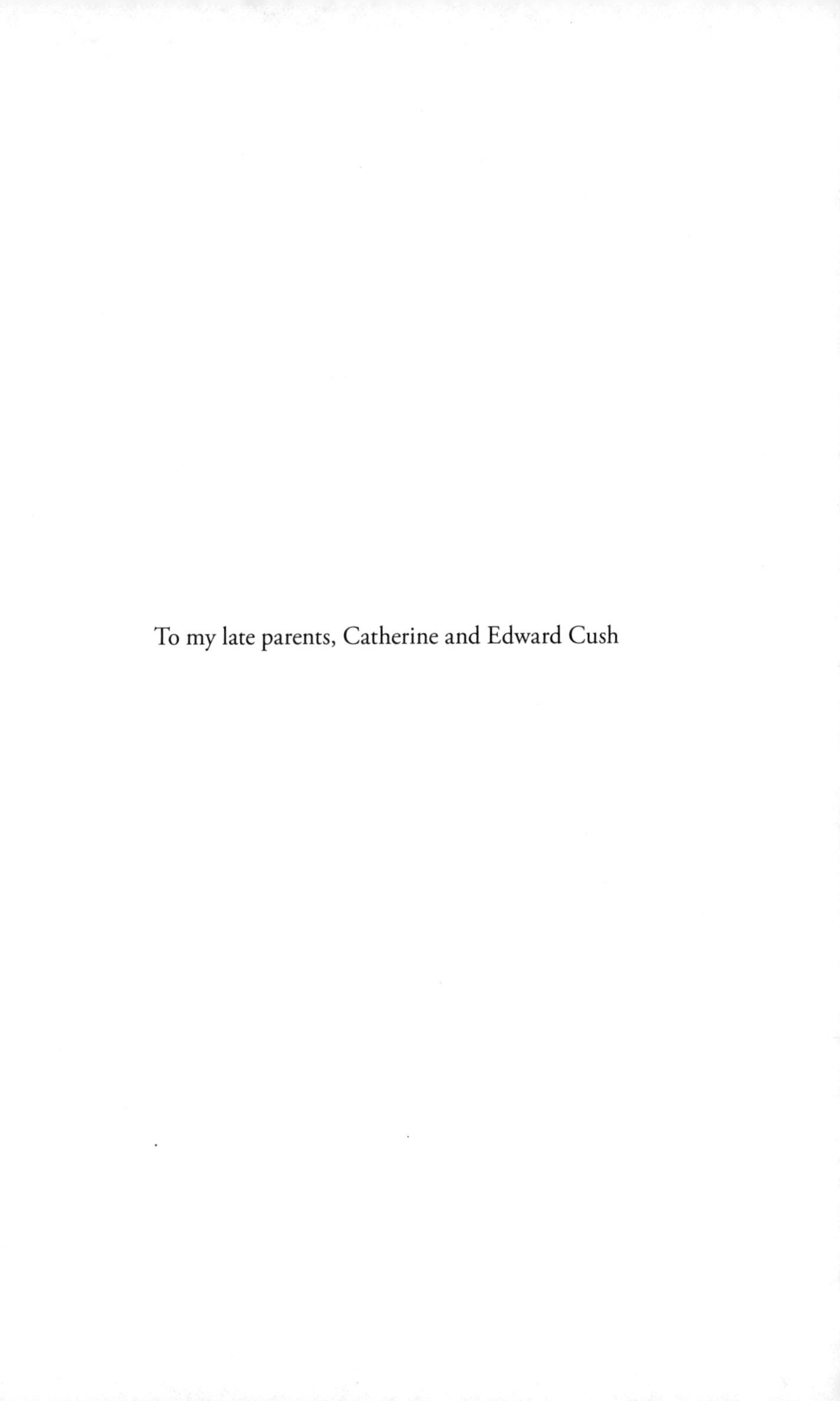

To my late parents, Catherine and Edward Cush

Contents

FOREWORD xi
Bishop John O. Barres

ACKNOWLEDGMENTS xvi

INTRODUCTION 1

PART I: PRIESTLY IDENTITY

INTRODUCTION TO PART I:
Set the World Ablaze 23

CHAPTER 1:
The Qualities of a Priest 26

CHAPTER 2:
Falling in Love with the Church, in Good Times and Bad:
A Hopeful Ecclesiology 51

CHAPTER 3:
Heroic Priesthood:
Priest as Mystagogue and Doctor of the Soul 76

PART II: PRIESTLY FORMATION

INTRODUCTION TO PART II:
The Four Dimensions of Priestly Formation 103

CHAPTER 4:
The Human Dimension 112

CHAPTER 5:
The Spiritual Dimension 137

CHAPTER 6:
The Intellectual Dimension 163

CHAPTER 7:
The Pastoral Dimension 193

CONCLUSION 222

Foreword

Bishop John O. Barres
Diocese of Rockville Centre

In a 2015 video message to an International Theological Congress held at the Pontifical Catholic University of Argentina, Pope Francis said:

> Not infrequently a kind of opposition is constructed between theology and pastoral care, as though they were two opposing, separate realities, which have nothing to do with one another. Not infrequently we identify doctrine with the conservative, the retrograde; and, on the contrary, we think that pastoral care is an adaptation, a reduction, an accommodation, as if they had nothing to do with one another. Thus, we create a false opposition between the so-called 'pastorally-minded' and the 'academics,' those on the side of the people and those on the side of doctrine. We create a false opposition between theology and pastoral care; between the believer's reflection and the believer's life; life, then, has no space for reflection and reflection finds no space in life. The great Fathers of the Church, Irenaeus, Augustine, Basil,

> Ambrose, to name a few, were great theologians because they were great pastors. One of the main contributions of the Second Vatican Council was precisely seeking a way to overcome this divorce between theology and pastoral care, between faith and life. I dare say that the Council has revolutionized to some extent the status of theology—the believer's way of doing and thinking.[1]

This statement is a great incentive for Catholic priests of all ages and in every season of their priesthood to actively and vibrantly study and integrate Catholic theology into their ever-expanding pastoral charity, their daily experience in evangelization, and the *ars celebrandi* of the liturgy. The priest is called to integrate Catholic theology and spirituality into his pastoral conversations in a natural way that uplifts, inspires, and helps form the people he is serving.

Bishop Robert Barron and Fr. John Cush follow in the line of Irenaeus, Augustine, Basil, Ambrose, and so many others to this day: they are fine theologians precisely because they are fine pastors and formators.

In *Nothing But You, Lord: Reflections on the Priesthood and Priestly Formation Through the Lens of Bishop Robert Barron*, Fr. Cush offers us a timely and insightful synthesis of Bishop Barron's theology and spirituality of the Catholic priesthood and the pastoral and formational artistry involved in forming twenty-first-century priests.

Fr. Cush combines a crisp, engaging, and clear writing style with theological acuity and precision. He draws on his vast experience as

1. Francis, "Video Message to Participants in an International Theological Congress Held at the Pontifical Catholic University of Argentina," September 3, 2015, vatican.va.

a priest, professor, and formator at the Pontifical North American College in Rome and St. Joseph's Seminary in New York in order to analyze Bishop Barron's unique contributions.

While surveying, synthesizing, and mining the vast range of Bishop Barron's books, documentaries, and podcasts, Fr. Cush insists it is "precisely through Bishop Barron's philosophical and theological acumen that he engages the world as effectively as any Catholic living today."

Bishop Barron's contributions to the theology and spirituality of the Catholic priesthood and to the twenty-first-century formation of Catholic priests—and Fr. Cush's valuable and insightful synthesis of these contributions—are a helpful compass as new models of seminary formation are discerned, tested, and implemented.

In taking seriously Avery Cardinal Dulles' 2004 McGinley Lecture, "The Rebirth of Apologetics," Bishop Barron has recognized with Cardinal Dulles that "apologetics has to meet the adversaries of the faith where they are in each successive generation."[2] In so doing, Bishop Barron has also heeded Pope Francis' call for a renewal of what the Holy Father calls "creative apologetics." In his 2013 apostolic exhortation, *Evangelii Gaudium*, Pope Francis writes:

> Proclaiming the Gospel message to different cultures also involves proclaiming it to professional, scientific, and academic circles. This means an encounter between faith, reason, and the sciences with a view to developing new approaches and arguments on the issue of credibility, a creative apologetics which would encourage

2. Avery Dulles, "The Rebirth of Apologetics," in *Church and Society: The Laurence J. McGinley Lectures, 1988–2007* (New York: Fordham University Press, 2008), 430–442.

> greater openness to the Gospel on the part of all. When certain categories of reason and the sciences are taken up into the proclamation of the message, these categories then become tools of evangelization; water is changed into wine. Whatever is taken up is not just redeemed, but becomes an instrument of the Spirit for enlightening and renewing the world.[3]

In his apostolic constitution on ecclesiastical universities and faculties, *Veritatis Gaudium*, Pope Francis calls for creative apologetics in universities. He writes, "It is to research conducted in ecclesiastical universities, faculties, and institutes that I primarily entrust the task of developing that 'creative apologetics' which I called for in *Evangelii Gaudium* [132] in order to 'encourage greater openness to the Gospel on the part of all.'"[4]

Bishop Barron has been at the forefront of the universal Church in responding to Pope Francis' call for a holistic pastoral and evangelizing accompaniment that includes the intellectual charity of creative apologetics. A commitment to a contemporary creative apologetics is critical to the pastoral, intellectual, and spiritual formation of twenty-first-century priests. Fr. Cush summarizes Bishop Barron's contribution well:

3. Francis, *Evangelii Gaudium* 132, apostolic exhortation, November 24, 2013, vatican.va.

4. Francis, *Veritatis Gaudium* 5, apostolic constitution, December 8, 2017, vatican.va. See also section 145 of the Pontifical Council for the Promotion of the New Evangelization's 2020 *Directory for Catechesis*: "*A knowledge of the discipline of apologetics*, which shows that faith is not opposed to reason and highlights the truths of a correct anthropology, illuminated by natural reason; the role of the *preambula fidei* is emphasized in order to '[develop] new approaches and arguments on the issue of credibility, a creative apologetics which would encourage greater openness to the Gospel on the part of all'" (Washington, DC: United States Conference of Catholic Bishops, 2020).

I am convinced that good theology leads to holiness of life, and holiness of life leads to a fruitful pastoral life of ministry and evangelization. Holiness of life also leads to good theology: this is demonstrated in the lives of St. Paul the Apostle, St. Augustine of Hippo, and St. Thomas Aquinas. In the present age, we can look to Pope St. John Paul II and Pope Benedict XVI. But too often today there is a gap between theology and sanctity, which means something is seriously wrong with either our theology or in the way we pursue sanctity. And I believe that making pastoral ministry fruitful by addressing this gap between theology and holiness of life is the goal of Bishop Barron. In my view, the fact that Barron has chosen to live his vocation as a Roman Catholic priest and bishop by embracing his role as a leading Catholic intellectual and theologian makes all the difference in the world to his ministry as an evangelist.

Acknowledgments

Without a doubt, I wish to express my thanks to the Most Reverend Robert E. Barron, Bishop of Winona-Rochester and founder of Word on Fire, for his priestly, evangelical, and theological inspiration to me as a priest and as a professor of theology.

This text could never have been completed without John B. Martino. John has been such a guide as proofreader and editor. I am amazed by his patience, his insight, and his kindness. He was, for me, like a doctor for this book, healing it when it was not looking too well. I was blessed to meet John and his family in person finally at the Academy of Catholic Theology held at the Dominican House of Studies, and yes, they are as super in person as John is via email!

The team at Word on Fire has been a joy to work with, and I cannot thank Brandon Vogt enough for inviting me to write this text, originally on the theology of Bishop Barron, but then helping me to focus more on the bishop's thoughts on priesthood and priestly formation. Jason Paone, David Augustine, Daniel Seseske, Matthew Becklo, and many others at Word on Fire have spent countless hours on this text to make it make sense and, hopefully, be an aid to my brother priests and seminarians.

This book stems from a number of articles that I wrote in 2019–2020 for the *National Catholic Register*, so I must thank Kevin Knight for his insights and kindness.

I am very grateful to His Excellency, the Most Reverend Robert J. Brennan, Bishop of Brooklyn, and his predecessor, the Most Reverend Nicholas DiMarzio, Bishop-Emeritus of Brooklyn, for their permission to write this text.

Thanks also must be given to the rectors, faculty, staff, and seminarians at the seminaries where I have served as a professor and formator, Saint Joseph's Seminary and College (Dunwoodie, New York) and the Pontifical North American College (Rome, Italy). To the Most Reverend James Massa, Rector, and our seminary community, please know of my sincere thanks for making Dunwoodie a home for me since 2022. To the Most Reverend James F. Checchio and Fr. Peter Harman, former Rectors of the Pontifical North American College, where I served on faculty from 2015–2022, my immense gratitude.

Introduction

On March 7, 2019, the Most Reverend Robert E. Barron, then auxiliary bishop of the Archdiocese of Los Angeles, stepped in front of a podium draped with a white cloth bearing the image of the papal keys. The auditorium was packed with students, guests, and professors, many of whom wore white and black habits—the traditional garb of the Order of Preachers founded by St. Dominic. This event was being held at the Pontifical University of Saint Thomas Aquinas ("the Angelicum") on the traditional feast day of its namesake saint as celebrated by his order.[1] Bishop Barron had come to Rome to receive an honorary doctorate from the Angelicum, which had been awarded after the Holy Mass earlier that day. Although auxiliary (literally "helper") bishops are rarely well known, most of those who awaited the bishop's lecture that day knew him as the founder of Word on Fire, a powerhouse organization for the promotion of the New Evangelization.

1. For those who know the current liturgical calendar of the Church, the choice of March 7 for the feast of St. Thomas Aquinas might seem rather odd since the current date assigned to the Angelic Doctor is January 28. The Dominican family of friars, nuns, and laity, however, still celebrate St. Thomas' feast day on the day he died, which was the date on the traditional Roman Catholic calendar.

The lecture that Bishop Barron delivered that day bore the title "The One Who Is; The One Who Gives: Aquinas, Derrida, and the Dilemma of the Divine Generosity."[2] From the opening line—"It is a favorite technique of those trained in the Derridean deconstructionist method . . ."—the bishop's erudition and insight came into full view. At the conclusion of the lecture, during which the bishop intricately interweaved his knowledge of Scholasticism and postmodern philosophy, one of my seminarians said to me, "Wow! I'm so used to Bishop Barron as an internet evangelist; I'd forgotten that he's a real systematic theologian too!"

That comment took me aback a bit, but I realized that it came from a common mindset. For some, including seminarians—and even, sadly, my brother priests—there's a disconnect between theology and the pastoral life. I have always tried in my own limited way as both a priest and professor to tie the formal study of theology to the pastoral life through the spiritual life of the pastor. I am convinced that good theology leads to holiness of life, and holiness of life leads to a fruitful pastoral life of ministry and evangelization. Holiness of life also leads to good theology; this is demonstrated in the lives of St. Paul the Apostle, St. Augustine of Hippo, and St. Thomas Aquinas. In the present age, we can look to Pope St. John Paul II and Pope Benedict XVI. But too often today there is a gap between theology and sanctity, which means something is seriously wrong with either our theology or in the way we pursue sanctity.

2. To view this lecture in its entirety, see the following link: Bishop Robert Barron, "The One Who Is; The One Who Gives," YouTube video, March 7, 2019, https://www.youtube.com/watch?v=FU83IZk4n8M. It is available in published form in Barron, "The One Who Is; The One Who Gives: Derrida, Aquinas, and the Dilemma of the Divine Generosity," in Barron, *Renewing Our Hope: Essays for the New Evangelization* (Washington, DC: The Catholic University of America Press, 2020), 97–113.

And I believe that making pastoral ministry fruitful by addressing this gap between theology and holiness of life is the goal of Bishop Barron. In my view, the fact that Barron has chosen to live his vocation as a Roman Catholic priest and bishop by embracing his role as a leading Catholic intellectual and theologian makes all the difference in the world to his ministry as an evangelist.

One way to show the importance of Bishop Barron's example is by way of a story from a time very early in my own priesthood. Now, I have to admit that I am not easily scandalized. Not to sound jaded or world-weary, but it takes an awful lot to shock me. And yet, a simple statement spoken clearly and directly by an older priest shook me to my very core. This priest stated—and unfortunately, not in jest—that, after his first three years as a priest, he had altogether ceased to write new homilies. After all, he had gone through the lectionary cycle, and, although the translation of the readings had changed over the years, the content of the readings had not. And so, for more than twenty years, Father had been reading the same now-yellowing sheets of handwritten paper at the pulpit, living off the fruits of his past labor. I was dumbfounded. I asked if he ever adapted them to the particular congregation to which he was preaching. He replied in the negative. I asked if he ever incorporated anything new that the Church had articulated, like papal encyclicals or the *Catechism of the Catholic Church*, since the first three years of his priesthood. And again, Father replied in the negative. Finally, I asked if he still read theology. He said he had not since he left the seminary. I believed him, because I looked around the priest's room where we sat and noticed that he had not a single book in his room. Not one!

Then, the words of a spiritual director from the college seminary that I attended came ringing back to my ears: "Beware the priest who has *no books* in his room, because he's probably not keeping up with his intellectual formation." This bookless priest was surely an extreme example, but it did drive home to me how priests really can just go on autopilot, at least as far as their intellectual life is concerned. Of course, just having books isn't enough either! Something else that same spiritual director said echoed in my mind: "Beware also the priest who has *lots of books* in the room if the binding is not cracked on any of them, because he has allowed himself to become just a book collector." So, I made a pledge to keep up with my intellectual formation as a young priest, and to not just be a *dilettante* who collected books and never really read them. I made a pledge to always try to update my homilies, even if some (or even most) of my thoughts on the Sunday readings remain the same three years later. And I have found that a priest must keep up his reading and study if he wishes to be an effective preacher and teacher of the Word and a vibrant minister of the altar. Of course, to avoid becoming like the Pharisee praying "I thank thee, God, that I am not like other men," I have to add that neglecting my books has not often been an option for me. For the majority of my priesthood, in one way or another, I have been involved in priestly formation: in the minor seminary, college-level seminary, pre-theologate, and major seminary. This is why I was in Rome for Bishop Barron's lecture, in fact!

Bishop Barron has likewise usually needed his books to fulfill his assignments, having been sent early in his priesthood for a doctorate at the Institut Catholique in Paris, France,[3] after which

3. The Doctor of Sacred Theology (abbreviated STD or SThD) is the final and highest academic degree awarded in Catholic universities that are part of the Pontifical system. A research

he was immediately assigned to Mundelein Seminary in his home archdiocese of Chicago. By 2010, he had published nine books and written many scholarly articles, but it was his budding work as an evangelist that was about to "go viral," with the release of a ten-part documentary titled *CATHOLICISM.* Within a few years, his ministry, Word on Fire, expanded and became a household name among plugged-in Catholics, and he had been raised first to the presidency of Mundelein Seminary and then the episcopate. Next was another documentary series beginning in 2016, *CATHOLICISM: The Pivotal Players*, about the great thinkers of the Catholic tradition. If any priest could claim to be too busy for the life of the mind, surely Bishop Barron had reached that point!

Yet despite all these responsibilities, since 2011, he has published many more books, including several with academic presses. If he no longer has the leisure to publish articles in scholarly journals, it is still his intelligent and insatiably curious engagement with the Catholic tradition and the contemporary culture that makes his evangelizing efforts stand out from the crowd. With each passing year, Bishop Barron has himself become a "pivotal player" in Catholicism, not only in the United States, but indeed around the world. The bishop is more than just an apologist and an evangelizer. He is a theologian *par excellence*. And he is a guiding light especially for priests for how to combine knowledge of the Word of God with a ministry to the people of God. Let me explain why.

degree, it is the equivalent of a PhD and has both ecclesiastical and academic ramifications. It takes around two to three years to complete.

BISHOP BARRON ON FIRE FOR THE INCARNATE WORD

I first heard of the bishop and his work from an article in the magazine *U.S. Catholic* in 1997. In that article, I encountered a very young Fr. Barron expounding his concept of the priest as "soul doctor." As a seminarian, I found this idea fascinating—so refreshing and radical. Next, I discovered his text *Thomas Aquinas: Spiritual Master* (1996). To me, as someone who is not especially trained in Thomistic thought, this book made Aquinas very appealing. At my ordination to the priesthood, an older priest gave me a copy of what is now my favorite of the bishop's books: *And Now I See: A Theology of Transformation* (1998). I still use both of these books in my classes in dogmatic and fundamental theology as exemplifying the kind of approach that I want my seminarians to take, one that is highly academic, deeply spiritual, and genuinely pastoral.

After those introductions, I have followed with interest the growth of Barron's ministry Word on Fire. Whether you read his books, watch his videos, or listen to his podcasts, he exudes the unbridled excitement of a student discovering or recalling some fascinating and invigorating truths. The "fire" of Word on Fire seems to me less like the spectacle of a bonfire in a crowd and more like the warm and crackling fire that invites one near for warmth, light, and a good chat. Yet this "fireside chat" style does not mean that he lacks zeal for souls—far from it. The passion that Bishop Barron exudes about *what* he is preaching or teaching stems, above all, from his excitement about *whom* he is really preaching: Jesus Christ. Bishop Barron does not believe in ideas only, but in a divine person. For him, Jesus is very real, and he is our Savior.

This love of Jesus is not based merely on sentiment; it is nourished by a profound reflection on who Jesus is, both in his humanity, which we share with him, and in his divinity, which he shares with us. And Barron argues that this fascination with an intelligent study of the mystery of the Incarnation is not only a personal quirk of his own; it is a fundamental feature of Christianity. In a review of Dominican Father Thomas Joseph White's 2015 book *The Incarnate Lord: A Thomistic Study in Christology*,[4] Barron writes, "This preoccupation with the being of Jesus signals, by the way, a major point of demarcation between Christianity and the other great religions of the world. Buddhists are massively interested in the teaching of the Buddha, but they are more or less indifferent to the ontology of the Buddha; no self-respecting Muslim worries about the existential make-up of Muhammad; and no Jew is preoccupied with the 'being' of Moses or Abraham."[5]

Barron observes that there was an attempt to submerge this question of Jesus' being at the time of his own theological formation during the 1980s, and he considers it to be one of the secret causes of the decline of the Church during and after that time. He contrasts the classical ontological approach with that of Friedrich Schleiermacher, a nineteenth-century Protestant theologian who influenced many of Barron's own professors.[6] Schleiermacher identified Jesus' divinity with "the constant potency of his God-consciousness," not the assumption of flesh by the Word of God, the Eternal Logos, who is born of the Father before all ages. Barron argues,

4. Thomas Joseph White, *The Incarnate Lord: A Thomistic Study in Christology* (Washington, DC: The Catholic University of America Press, 2015).

5. Robert Barron, "Why It Matters Who Jesus Is," Word on Fire, March 14, 2017, https://www.wordonfire.org/resources/article/why-it-matters-who-jesus-is/5412/.

6. Friedrich Schleiermacher (1768–1834) was a German Protestant theologian who has been called "The Father of Modern Liberal Theology."

> The abandonment of an ontological approach has myriad negative consequences, but I will focus on just a few. First, it effectively turns Jesus into a type of super-saint, different perhaps in degree from other holy people, but not in kind. Hence, on this reading, it is not the least bit clear why Jesus is of any greater significance than other religious figures and founders. If he is a saint, even a great one, well people can argue so is Confucius, so is the Buddha, so are the Sufi mystics and Hindu sages, and so in their own way are Socrates, Walt Whitman, and Albert Schweitzer. If Jesus mediates the divine to you, well and good, but why should you feel any particular obligation to propose him to someone else, who is perhaps more moved by a saintly person from another religious tradition? Indeed, if "God-consciousness" is the issue, who are we to say that Jesus' was any wider or deeper than St. Francis' or Mother Teresa's? In a word, the motivation for real evangelization more or less dissipates when one navigates the Schleiermacher highway.[7]

There is no question that Barron himself is motivated to real evangelization, and this drive cannot be abstracted from his belief in Jesus as "infinity dwindled to infancy," to borrow the title of a book written by Fr. Edward T. Oakes, a late colleague of Barron's at Mundelein.[8] And this ontologically rich understanding of Jesus grounds his notion of the ministry of the Church in which he lives out his priesthood. Barron writes,

7. Robert Barron, "Why It Matters Who Jesus Is."

8. Edward T. Oakes, *Infinity Dwindled to Infancy: A Catholic and Evangelical Christology* (Grand Rapids, MI: Eerdmans, 2011). Fr. Oakes actually takes the phrase "infinity dwindled to infancy" from Gerard Manly Hopkins' poem "The Blessed Virgin compared to the Air we Breathe." Hopkins (1844–1889) is one of Bishop Barron's favorite poets.

> More fundamentally, when the stress is placed on Jesus' human consciousness of God, the spiritual weight falls overwhelmingly on the side of immanence. What I mean is our quest for God, our search for the divine, and our growth in spiritual awareness become paramount, rather than what God has uniquely accomplished and established. When the Church says that Jesus *is* God, she means that the divine life, through the graceful intervention of God, has become available to the world in an utterly unique manner. She furthermore means that she herself—in her preaching, her formal teaching, in her sacraments, and in her saints—is the privileged vehicle through which this life now flows into human hearts and into the culture. It is easy enough to see that the transition from an ontological Christology to a consciousness Christology has conduced toward all manner of relativism, subjectivism, indifferentism, and the attenuation of evangelical zeal.[9]

Bishop Barron thus teaches us—priests in particular—to hold fast to "the priority of Christ" (the title of one of his most important books).[10] Christology (who Jesus is) informs soteriology (how Jesus saves us), which informs ecclesiology (who we are as the Church, the Mystical Body of Christ, the Bride of Christ, the People of God), finally influencing theological anthropology (who we are as human beings in light of God).[11] Bishop Barron does not see any of these

9. Barron, "Why It Matters Who Jesus Is."

10. Robert Barron, *The Priority of Christ: Toward a Postliberal Catholicism* (Grand Rapids, MI: Baker Academic, 2007).

11. For concise definitions of academic theological terms, see John P. Cush, *The How-To Book of Catholic Theology: Everything You Need to Know but No One Ever Taught You* (Huntington, IN: Our Sunday Visitor, 2020).

topics as simply academic subjects that can be surmounted and then set aside by priests in favor of pastoral ministry in the "real world." As a priest, the notion of who Jesus is has to be central in my life of prayer and service. If I am to be, by my ordination, an *alter Christus* (another Christ), I must strive to understand who Jesus is. Only then can I serve in Jesus' name as his priest.

BISHOP BARRON AS A PRIEST AND BISHOP FOR THE WORLD

But doesn't all this focus on the mind of the priest pose a danger to his pastoral heart? In 1 Corinthians 8:1, St. Paul cautions, "Knowledge puffs up, but love builds up." There is indeed a danger of a divided heart among priests, but this has less to do with prayerful and careful thinking about the mysteries of faith, and more about piling up "expertise" and its associated prestige and overexertion. When I was a seminarian in the college-level seminary, the spiritual director emphatically warned us about the danger of being a "hyphenated priest," such as a priest-professor, a priest-psychologist, or a priest-lawyer. To this list he might have added "priest–internet evangelist," even though such a figure scarcely existed when I was a seminarian! The primary duty of a priest is to be the minister of the sacraments and the Word. Yet it's not unusual for priests to be asked or commanded to have a secondary apostolate by their religious order, their diocesan bishop, or even a special inspiration of the Holy Spirit. Was this spiritual director telling us to disobey those promptings and focus only on the "regular" work of a priest?

As St. Paul likes to say, "By no means!" Rather, he was making the point that no matter his apostolate, the priest should recall that he is a priest before all else. And it is this priority of the priesthood of Christ that I also observe in Bishop Barron's activities, no matter how numerous. Bishop Barron's own priesthood is not merely a trapping; it is more than just the clerical attire that he wears or the ecclesiastical titles he holds. To listen to him speak, to see him teach, to watch him offer the Holy Sacrifice of the Mass, one can sense that each activity is an act of love given to the One whom he loves and in service of the One who loves him. No one who meets Bishop Barron can doubt the central place the priesthood occupies in his life; it is first and primary. It is who he is, and it informs what he does.

But one could still object that too much focus on the distinctive, highly complex theology of the Church—regarding Christ, the Trinity, and even the priesthood itself—will cut a priest off from his twenty-first-century people. Are we not living in an age known more for emotion than reason, for tolerance than truth, for endless seeking than solid answers? Would it not resonate more with our contemporaries to focus on more basic claims like the goodness of God, the fraternity of men and women, and the importance of doing good for the poor, rather than what it means for the Father to be "consubstantial" with the Son or for the Church of Christ to "subsist in" the Catholic Church? To put it another way: Instead of focusing on the exclusive and excessively intellectual claims of Catholic identity, should we not seek whatever common ground we can find with all people of good will so as to remain relevant?

Bishop Barron's own popularity responds to this objection, though, as it's precisely *through* his philosophical and theological acumen that he engages the world as effectively as any Catholic living today. His approach amounts to more, of course, than a bland restatement of the ancient teachings of the tradition. Rather, Barron's success owes much to the way that he presents the timeless wisdom of the tradition in dialogue with contemporary culture and thought. Through dialogue in this way, Barron navigates between the horns of the dilemma that Christians face in secular cultural contexts wherein being "relevant" often involves shedding the most distinctive features of our identity and tradition. In his discussion of Rod Dreher's book *The Benedict Option: A Strategy for Christians in a Post-Christian Nation*, Barron comments on this dilemma:

> The more we emphasize the uniqueness of Christianity, the less, it seems, the faith speaks to the wider culture; and the more we emphasize the connection between faith and culture, the less distinctive, it seems, Christianity becomes. This problem is on display throughout church history, as the society becomes, by turns, more or less amenable to the faith. In the era when I was coming of age, the period just after the Council, the Church was thoroughly committed to relevance, so committed in fact that it came close to losing its identity completely.[12]

Barron agrees that the Church must be in dialogue with the contemporary world, but he points to St. John Paul II as a model who "struck such a dynamic balance between the poles." He asks rhetorically, "Who was more of an ardent defender of distinctive, colorful, confident Catholicism than the Polish Pope? But at the same time, who was more committed to reaching out to the non-Christian world, to secularism, to atheism than he?"[13] As a young man involved

12. Bishop Robert Barron, "The Benedict Option and the Identity/Relevance Dilemma," Word on Fire, April 18, 2017, https://www.wordonfire.org/resources/article/the-benedict-option-and-the-identity-relevance-dilemma/5442/.

13. Barron, "The Benedict Option and the Identity/Relevance Dilemma."

in theater and the arts, the future pope helped to preserve Poland's cultural identity even in the face of foreign oppression. However, as the young Karol Wojtyła grew into his priestly vocation, "he was properly prepared to unleash the energy he had stored. The result was one of the most dramatic transformations of society in modern history. Better than almost anyone in the Church at the time, he knew how to make the ancient faith relevant to the culture."[14]

When Bishop Barron reviews a film or a contemporary book, he is not "kowtowing to a fallen and corrupt culture," as some would have it, but is instead practicing the wisdom of viewing all things in the light of Christ. This is, in fact, a deeply Catholic thing to do, hearkening back to St. Ignatius of Loyola and, even further, to St. Paul the Apostle. When Bishop Barron gave his talk at the Googleplex in Mountain View, California, on March 20, 2018,[15] it was not a vain attempt at relevancy; on the contrary, it was his way of fulfilling his mission and his vocation as a Catholic believer and, as a bishop, a modern-day successor of the Apostles.

On YouTube, X (formerly Twitter), and Facebook, Barron is entering into a modern-day Areopagus, a place full of enthusiastic confusions, endlessly warring philosophies, and cynical sophistry. What St. Paul sought in that ancient Greek forum for debate was not those who already had the right answers, but those who had questions. We read in Acts 17 that most of the Athenians present dismissed or mocked Paul, but some wanted to hear more, and a few

14. Barron, "The Benedict Option and the Identity/Relevance Dilemma."

15. Bishop Robert Barron, "Religion and the Opening Up of the Mind (Google Talk)," Word on Fire, March 20, 2018, https://www.wordonfire.org/resources/lecture/religion-and-the-opening-up-of-the-mind-google-talk/5770/. For the published form of this talk, see Barron, *Arguing Religion: A Bishop Speaks at Facebook and Google* (Park Ridge, IL: Word on Fire, 2018), 59–106.

even became disciples. When he addresses the secular, Bishop Barron never loses sight of the sacred. He can do this because—despite all his respect for culture and for every person's experience—he never *reduces* his engagement *to* culture and experience. He always keeps the wider ontological horizon in view, just as he did at that podium in Rome when he showed how the metaphysics of Christ as explained by Thomas Aquinas can make possible real generosity, despite the postmodern objections of a Jacques Derrida. The truth, in the hands of Bishop Barron, is not a citadel to be protected but a light that shines. And his knowledge and his sincerity are recognized by those whom he encounters, as is his abiding faith in Christ and his Church.

THE PURPOSE AND STRUCTURE OF THIS BOOK

Following this introduction, the book you are holding (or scrolling through) is divided into two parts on the topics of priestly identity and priestly formation. You might ask: Why begin with priestly identity? The term "identity" has become an awfully loaded one in our culture, with the clashes of "identity-driven politics" and new claims about "gender identity." Obviously, what I don't mean in talking about "priestly identity" is "identity politics"—that is, one group of people promoting their interests over and against some other group. Some priests do think of themselves over and against the laity—and this is called clericalism, which is rightly condemned today. Nor do I mean something the priest just feels deep inside to be true about himself, which is how gender identity claims are often put forward. Rather, I mean something objective, a free gift from God that comes through the sacrament of Holy Orders. In other words, priestly identity comes from priestly character, the unique configuration to the person of Jesus given to each of us unworthy recipients as a grace for us and, through us, the whole Church.

Why not just say "priestly character" then? I think it's important to speak of identity, because priestly character, which is given by God, cannot be lost, but priests certainly can be confused in their sense of their own identity, like the hyphenated priests I mentioned earlier. Until you really know and comprehend who you are, in the ultimate sense, you cannot at all understand what you are to do! In any case, I am following John Paul II, who spoke specifically of a "crisis of priestly identity" that he was responding to in the current foundational document of priestly formation, *Pastores Dabo Vobis*. At the 1990 synod of bishops that led to that document, the saintly pope addressed the gathered episcopate in the following words:

> This crisis arose in the years immediately following the Council. It was based on an erroneous understanding of—and sometimes even a conscious bias against—the doctrine of the conciliar magisterium. Undoubtedly, herein lies one of the reasons for the great number of defections experienced then by the Church, losses which did serious harm to pastoral ministry and priestly vocations, especially missionary vocations. It is as though the 1990 synod—rediscovering, by means of the many statements which we heard in this hall, the full depth of priestly identity—has striven to instill hope in the wake of these sad losses. These statements showed an awareness of the specific ontological bond which unites the priesthood to Christ the high priest and good shepherd. This identity is built upon the type of formation which

> must be provided for priesthood and then endure throughout the priest's whole life. This was the precise purpose of the synod.[16]

In my own personal experience, this crisis is not over, even thirty years later, and the lack of a full rediscovery of priestly identity is the single greatest obstacle for priests today. Is the priest the shepherd of souls? Is he the chief catechist of his parish? Is he the sacramental minister? Is he the coordinator of the ministries of others? Is he the CEO of a small local business, or middle-management in a corporation called "the Catholic Church"? Into this cacophony of role confusion, Bishop Barron first draws us back to the basics—which is to say, who Christ is, who the Church is, and therefore who the priest ordered to Christ and in service of the Church is. The ministerial priesthood is rooted in the priesthood of all the baptized, and it is based on the fundamental marks of the Church identified in the creed. I will identify the essential characteristics of a priest and demonstrate the importance of a formation pedagogy that conveys an accurate understanding of the nature of a priest to priests in training.

In chapter 1, we will look to the triple *munera* (offices) of Christ (priest, prophet, king) into which all Christians are baptized, and explore the unique way that an ordained priest participates in these *munera*. For a concrete example, we will consider how Bishop Barron's own ministry exhibits these *munera*. In the second chapter, we will look at the priest in relation to the nature of the Church, describing the necessity of falling in love with the Bride of Christ

16. John Paul II, *Pastores Dabo Vobis* 11, citing the "Discourse at the End of the Synod" 4; cf. "Letter to Priests for Holy Thursday 1991," March 10, 1991 (*L'Osservatore Romano*, March 15, 1991).

and being in harmony with her—especially now, in this time of uncertainty and crisis. Finally, in chapter 3, we will discuss the desired end of all priestly formation according to Bishop Barron's unique formulations—namely, being a heroic priest who is engaged in his ministry as both a mystagogue and a doctor of the soul.

These last two concepts—the priest as doctor of the soul and mystagogue—can lead us to a greater understanding of who a priest is and what a priest is supposed to do. I have written this book because I believe, from my own experience as a priest, that Robert Barron's writings offer the Church a very good roadmap for how to reach a place of fruitful ministry for the priest of the twenty-first century.[17] I believe that, if applied correctly and in accord with the rest of the vision that the Church sets out concerning priestly formation, Barron's thought can be a powerful addition to a contemporary understanding of priesthood, one that seeks to offer a holistic approach to the life of the priest. I hope that it will not only help orient priests in their ministry, but also help the laity who pick up this book to understand how they can help their priests and what they should and should not expect from them.

Once we have these fundamental signposts of identity clear from the first three chapters, the second part of the book concerns how a man should be formed into such a priest. This second half is organized around the aforementioned *Pastores Dabo Vobis* ("I Will Give You Shepherds"), a post-synodal apostolic exhortation promulgated by Pope St. John Paul II in 1992. This foundational document establishes four dimensions of priestly formation: human

17. It must be stated that the application and interpretation of Bishop Barron's theology is solely my own interpretation and should not be considered the official word of Bishop Barron or of Word on Fire.

formation, which is the bedrock on which all other developments rest; spiritual formation, in which a man centers his life on Christ and Christ alone; intellectual formation, in which a man develops the cultural, historical, philosophical, and, above all, theological tools to serve as a priest; and finally, pastoral formation, where in a very real sense "the rubber hits the road," as a man applies the fruit of what he has developed in the other three dimensions. I will also refer to *Ratio Fundamentalis Sacerdotalis* (2016) and the USCCB's *Program of Priestly Formation* (2022).

BEGINNING THIS JOURNEY

Every priest, no matter his assignment, should care deeply about the formation of his future brother priests. Each priest, not just the vocations director, impacts vocations, because each is a walking ad for the priesthood, for the Church, for Christ, for God. At no time is this more apparent than when the priest wears his clerical attire in public. When a priest wears his collar, his presence is no longer about him; it's about the faith he represents—for good or ill! But the goal, as should by now be clear, is not to put on a good show or to paint a false, rosy picture of priestly life in the way that many advertisers try to sell their products. The goal is to be unafraid to live priestly identity! And as John Paul II might say, it is "a gift and a task."

The task of priestly formation is not a matter of concern to priests alone either. Poor priestly formation spills out into the people of God in small and frustrating—and sometimes deeply tragic—ways. Just as I hope that Catholic families, parishes, and organizations will pray and work to encourage young (and not so young!) men to find their vocations, I hope that lay readers of this book will have a better idea of what does and should go into the fostering of those vocations after those men enter formation. As Bishop Barron observes, "A better and stronger laity shapes a better and stronger (and less clericalist) priesthood."[18] "The bottom line is this: if we want holier priests, we all have to become holier ourselves."[19]

As we begin this journey reading about the priesthood, I ask you to call to mind the priests whom you know. Bring them into your consciousness and thought. Recall all of them: the ones who have inspired you; the ones who have comforted you; the ones who have given you the Bread of Life, Jesus Christ, in the Eucharist; the ones who have absolved your sins in the sacrament of Penance. Recall also the ones who have let you down; the ones who have brushed you off; the ones who have sinned; and even the ones who have left the ministry, either by their own choice, or who, due to horrific crimes, have been dismissed from the clerical state. And I, as a priest myself, ask one favor on behalf of all of my brother priests: pray for us! Pray for all of us who are out there in this world, believing in God, believing in Christ, believing in his Church, living out our baptismal call as priests. And please pray, too, for priestly vocations. We don't just need more priests. It's not about quantity; it's about quality. I'd rather have one well-formed man ordained than ten who have floated half-heartedly through the seminary, never allowing themselves to be known by their formators, by their peers, or even by themselves. We need priests who are happy and healthy (human formation), striving for holiness (spiritual formation), and intelligent interlocutors with the world (intellectual formation), so that they can go and be the presence of Christ in the world (pastoral ministry).

18. Barron, *Renewing Our Hope,* 93.

19. Bishop Robert Barron, *Letter to a Suffering Church: A Bishop Speaks on the Sexual Abuse Crisis* (Park Ridge, IL: Word on Fire, 2019), 92.

May Mary and Joseph, who helped to educate Jesus for his earthly ministry, remain close to us as we ponder in our hearts again the mysteries of his Word: “The harvest is plentiful, but the laborers are few; therefore ask the Lord of the harvest to send out laborers into his harvest” (Matt. 9:37–38).

PART I

Priestly Identity

INTRODUCTION TO PART I

Set the World Ablaze

In the summer of 2016, I had just finished my first year on the formation faculty of the Pontifical North American College in Rome when I was asked by my seminary's rector to attend a program for seminary formators at Creighton University in Omaha, Nebraska. One day, I took a long walk around campus and found an impressive monument, appropriate for a Jesuit university: a perpetual flame with an inscription of the words of the founder of the Society of Jesus, St. Ignatius of Loyola: "Ite Inflammate Omnia"—"Go, set the world ablaze." These words, of course, were inspired by the words of the Lord Jesus taken from Luke 12:49 (NABRE): "I have come to set the earth on fire, and how I wish it were already blazing!" Being inflamed with the love of the Lord should be the goal of each and every Christian. By our words and actions, we need to set the earth on fire! And yet, if we were to go to some parishes on a Sunday, being on fire for the Lord would be the last thing of which we as Catholics, especially some of us who are ordained ministers of the Gospel, would be accused.

Why are we falling short thus far? Perhaps it is partly because "to set fire to the earth" is not only "splendid in its beauty" but also "terrifying and dangerous," as Bishop Barron testifies based on his own experience of the 2018 wildfires in his then-diocese of Los Angeles, California.[1] Fire gives needed warmth and light, but it also destroys and purifies. Consider Jesus' disturbing prophecy in the verses in Luke that quickly follow his exclamation about setting the earth on fire: "Do you think that I have come to bring peace to the earth? No, I tell you, but rather division! From now on five in one household will be divided, three against two and two against three; they will be divided: father against son and son against father, mother against daughter and daughter against mother, mother-in-law against her daughter-in-law and daughter-in-law against mother-in-law" (Luke 12:51–53).

Jesus speaks in this way, the bishop explains, because our world is "off-kilter," "marked by selfishness, stupidity, violence, and cruelty." To such a world, even though the Word made flesh is its goal and fulfillment, Jesus "appears as a threat . . . a disruption, a sign of contradiction." Jesus' goal, of course, is definitely not division or even purification for its own sake, but for the sake of what comes afterward: new life and growth for those who accept it. But this transformation requires him "to burn some things out, to clear some things out, to force some people out of their tranquil domesticity."[2]

Bishop Barron calls us out of a dull, domesticated faith, what he often calls "beige Catholicism," to a fully supernatural vision of truth. We should be on fire because we recognize the message, the basic kerygma—"Christ has died, Christ has risen, Christ will come

1. Robert Barron, "A Light Unto My Path: Twentieth Sunday in Ordinary Time," *Magnificat* (August 2022): 180. Being discouraged by scandals and confused about our identity are other reasons for lukewarmness, but I will discuss those in later chapters.

2. Barron, 180.

again"[3] —has become ours through a death like his in Baptism. We share in the eternal life that is our Lord, Jesus Christ. We are washed clean in the Precious Blood of the Lamb of God, who has come to take our sins away. We are made in Christ a new creation.

How can we reignite the fire with which the Lord has blessed us, first of all within us priests? How can we keep it lit in response to the "wind and waves . . . that threaten us on the journey"?[4] As I explained in the introduction, Bishop Barron cautions us that we will not sustain ourselves on the "experiential and emotional" alone without opening our hearts and minds to the "intellectual" aspects of faith.[5] Consider an old axiom from St. Thomas Aquinas: "You cannot love what you do not know." Let's apply this axiom to priests. How can we grow to love the Lord, the Church, and our unique vocations more? By seeking "the things that are above," as St. Paul tells the Colossians, not what is on earth (Col. 3:1). This means using our intellects to see through the surface activity of ordained ministry and to peer into the depths, the ontology of these great mysteries that we bear "in earthen vessels" (2 Cor. 4:7 NABRE). In these three chapters, following Bishop Barron's lead, I'll explore the threefold *munera* of Christ and how they shape the priesthood, the marks of the Church and their relation to the priesthood, and the unique call of the priest as mystagogue and doctor of the soul. As Jesus indicates, living the priesthood so as to set the world on fire will not be without its tribulations, but we can take heart, for he has overcome the world.

3. As we said in the former translation of the Mass in English.

4. Robert Barron, *The Strangest Way: Walking the Christian Path* (Park Ridge, IL: Word on Fire Institute, [2008] 2021), 48.

5. Robert Barron, *Renewing Our Hope: Essays for the New Evangelization* (Washington, DC: The Catholic University of America Press, 2020), 18.

CHAPTER I

The Qualities of a Priest

The importance of "setting the earth on fire" to Bishop Barron is evident in the title of his 2017 interview book with John L. Allen Jr., *To Light a Fire on the Earth: Proclaiming the Gospel in a Secular Age* (2017). In this interview, Bishop Barron describes how his own heart was first set aflame thanks to his experience with the Dominican Friars at Fenwick High School in Oak Park, Illinois.[1] His youthful encounter with the Catholic intellectual tradition—especially St. Thomas Aquinas—opened a whole new world for him intellectually and spiritually, and formed a foundation for the priestly vocation that he would later discern. I know many readers cannot relate to this experience of high school, but I can. At my Catholic high school in New York, I experienced a real awakening in my spiritual life and in my academic endeavors, and I met some wonderful priests who encouraged me to take my faith seriously, to be open to a priestly vocation, and to cultivate a voracious desire to learn everything the Western cultural tradition had to offer. My

1. Robert Barron with John L. Allen Jr., *To Light a Fire on the Earth: Proclaiming the Gospel in a Secular Age* (New York: Image Books, 2017), 18–20.

high school years changed the way I viewed the world, the way I saw the Church, the way I saw the priesthood, and the way I saw myself.

Too many people think of Christianity as merely something one does, either a set of ritual activities or a moral code. By contrast, Bishop Barron, in his masterpiece *And Now I See: A Theology of Transformation*, states, "Christianity is, above all, a way of *seeing*. Everything else in Christian life flows from and circles around the transformation of vision. Christians *see* differently, and that is why their prayer, their worship, their action, and their whole way of being in the world have a distinctive accent and flavor."[2] Our way of seeing the world is quietly shaped throughout our childhood, but high school in particular is a formative, educational period in which a young adult forms a conscious perspective that will often mark his or her path long into adulthood. Thus, I always tell people that the work of forming flourishing priests begins not at seminary or in vocation outreach but much earlier, with the task of forming people with a splendidly Christian view of the world. The formation of priests best begins with the formation of young persons—through good families, of course, but also through the kind of well-rounded education that imparts this vision. Within the context of this sort of Christian formation, one can begin to discern the call to a priestly vocation.

Unfortunately, as Bishop Barron has observed on many occasions, "over the past several decades, at least in the West, there has been an extraordinary dumbing down of the faith." While he lays some of the blame on liberal theology, as I discussed in the

2. Robert Barron, *And Now I See: A Theology of Transformation* (Park Ridge, IL: Word on Fire Academic, [1998] 2021), xi.

introduction, Barron also attributes "much of it" to "a stubborn insistence that religion is not something that young people ought to be thinking about seriously." Instead,

> Other priorities—community, the sharing of feelings, a commitment to social justice—all outweighed the importance of theology. Why do our high school students, in Catholic schools, read Shakespeare in English class, Einstein in physics class, Virgil in Latin class—but elementary books in religion? If young people can handle Shakespeare, Einstein, and Virgil, why in the world couldn't they handle Augustine, Aquinas, and Chesterton? Why in so many of our religious education programs and Confirmation preparation programs is there little focused study of the Creed, or no apologetic engagement with the objections to the faith which are on offer so widely in our culture?[3]

Hence, supporting more robust educational and catechetical approaches—and schools and parishes that embody this intellectual seriousness—is a great way to encourage vocations to the priesthood and ultimately build up better priests.

But I'm very aware that many men considering or entering the priesthood have not had this early formative experience. Some are able to get it from a subsequent college experience. Some find a ministry like the Fellowship of Catholic University Students (FOCUS), the Alliance for Catholic Education, or the Thomistic Institute that helps them see reality in a Christian light despite other influences

3. Robert Barron, *Renewing Our Hope: Essays for the New Evangelization* (Washington, DC: The Catholic University of America Press, 2020), 18.

from a contrary education. Others have to piece their Christian education together for themselves at a later date. I don't have the space in this book to lay out a comprehensive reading list for young men who want to "catch up" on a liberal education, although the reader could pick up my book *The How-To Book of Catholic Theology* for some starting points in theology at least.[4] Another avenue would be to read not only Bishop Barron but all of the great sources that are shared and recommended through Word on Fire, not only in theology, but in philosophy, literature, film, and so on.

Does this mean, though, that only "nerds" or "geeks" are suitable for the priesthood? By no means! After some years of serving as a seminary formator (and even more years of being a seminarian myself), I can say that when you have met one seminarian, you have met one seminarian! Each person is unique. Some enjoy sports, and some do not; some are interested in films, and some are not; and the list goes on and on. However, I think that there are four important traits that every seminarian should possess: first, an openness to the workings of the Lord; second, a prayerful spirit; third, an openness to growing in the intellectual understanding of the faith; and fourth, a desire to serve.

These correspond to the four areas in which they'll be expected to grow as seminarians: human formation, spiritual formation, intellectual formation, and pastoral formation. In his human development, the man discerning a vocation to the priesthood does not need to be a Renaissance man or a paragon of natural virtue; he just needs to realize that "his life is not about him," as Bishop

4. John P. Cush, *The How-To Book of Catholic Theology: Everything You Need to Know but No One Ever Taught You* (Huntington, IN: Our Sunday Visitor, 2020).

Barron likes to say. The potential priest does not need to be a spiritual master, but he should, even at the start, at least want to pray (or want to want to pray).[5] He does not need to be a scholar, but he needs to recognize that his long years of study will be worthwhile as the foundation for his pastoral ministry.[6] And he does not need to already be thoroughly selfless, but unless he shows potential to be a happy giver in all areas of his life—including the most intimate part of himself, his own chastity—it is difficult to expect that he will ever be fulfilled as a priest.

The foundation of his priesthood is thus living the life of a baptized believer. We might elucidate the key aspects of this life in the Rite of Baptism itself. Immediately following the Baptism by water, the officiating priest or deacon anoints the newly baptized with chrism oil and declares, "Almighty God, the Father of our Lord Jesus Christ, has freed you from sin, given you new birth by water and the Holy Spirit, and joined you to his people. He now anoints you with the Chrism of salvation, so that you may remain members of Christ, Priest, Prophet and King, unto eternal life."[7] The liturgy thus declares that every baptized Christian shares in Christ's life through Baptism, and thereby participates in his priestly, prophetic, and royal missions. The *Catechism of the Catholic Church* further explains the distinct ways in which the laity and clergy participate in Christ's threefold mission:

5. If over time he does not have a desire both for personal prayer and to offer the Holy Sacrifice of the Mass each day—not only for himself but for the sake of the longing world—as a formator I would encourage him to re-evaluate his vocational choice.

6. This is a particular point of emphasis for me, which I will discuss in the chapter on intellectual formation.

7. *Rite of Baptism for Children* 98.

> The ministerial or hierarchical priesthood of bishops and priests, and the common priesthood of all the faithful participate, "each in its own proper way, in the one priesthood of Christ." While being "ordered one to another," they differ essentially. In what sense? While the common priesthood of the faithful is exercised by the unfolding of baptismal grace—a life of faith, hope, and charity, a life according to the Spirit—the ministerial priesthood is at the service of the common priesthood. It is directed at the unfolding of the baptismal grace of all Christians.[8]

Hence, all Christians enter into Christ's triple *munera*, but certain Christians are called to conform their lives more specifically to Christ's, and thus to assume his threefold mission in a new and special way. In "Matrimony and Holy Orders," the sixth episode in his series *The Sacraments*, Bishop Barron—echoing the constant teaching of the Church—insists that those in Holy Orders must conform themselves to Christ in the entirety of their being. This calling entails that they serve the Church (and the world) in the way Christ does.

Consequently, as Fr. Philip-Michael F. Tangorra explains, "A priest is one who offers sacrifice on behalf of others," as Jesus did. And as Jesus instructed the world in the manner of a prophet, a priest likewise "teaches others the way they should live, so as to avoid evil and embrace the good." Finally, Jesus came not only to sacrifice and to teach but also as a king to establish his heavenly kingdom in love. Similarly, a priest "governs and uses his authority so that others may be brought into the fulness of their potential. The gift of authority,

8. *Catechism of the Catholic Church* 1547.

in the Church, is only properly used when it is employed to build up the Church, and grow the kingdom of God, which is like a seed [see Matt. 13:31]."[9]

In the following sections, I will explore what it means for an ordained priest to share in these *munera*, this threefold mission of Jesus Christ the Lord, by studying each mission—priestly, prophetic, and kingly—in turn.

BEING A PRIEST

All Christians participate in the priesthood of Christ by virtue of their Baptism. If someone walks into a Catholic Church and asks, "Where is the priest?" you could honestly point to everyone in the pews and say, "They're right here!" Every Christian is called, as St. Paul says, "to offer your bodies as a living sacrifice, holy and pleasing to God, your spiritual worship" (Rom. 12:1). For example, there are wonderful groups like the Serra Clubs who commit themselves to pray specifically for priestly and religious vocations—and we sure need such groups today, when so many families sadly do not encourage their children to consider service to the Church. Whether or not they belong to such a group, all Catholics form part of a society that gathers to lift up their hearts and minds to the Lord for the sake of the world—because we do it at every Mass! As a priest, I say it in every liturgy: *Orate, fratres, ut meum ac vestrum sacrificium acceptabile fiat apud Deum Patrem omnipotentem* ("Pray, brethren, that *my* sacrifice and *yours* may be acceptable to God, the almighty Father").

9. Philip-Michael F. Tangorra, "Jesus Christ: Priest, Prophet, and King," *Homiletics and Pastoral Review*, October 25, 2013, https://www.hprweb.com/2013/10/jesus-christ-priest-prophet-and-king/.

Nevertheless, a man begins to participate in Christ's priesthood in a new and fuller way, called the "high priesthood," when he is ordained by a bishop in the sacrament of Holy Orders.[10] The bishop's essential role in the sacrament that transforms a candidate for priesthood into a priest indicates the nature of the relationship between bishops and priests. It would be a mistake to understand a bishop as though he were a priest with an additional supervisory role. Rather, the bishop is the original and primary bearer of the high priesthood in which priests participate as "assistants."[11]

> Episcopal consecration, together with the office of sanctifying, also confers the office of teaching and of governing, which, however, of its very nature, can be exercised only in hierarchical communion with the head and the members of the college. . . . By means of the imposition of hands and the words of consecration, the grace of the Holy Spirit is so conferred, and the sacred character so impressed, that bishops in an eminent and visible way sustain the roles of Christ Himself as Teacher, Shepherd, and High Priest, and that they act in His person. Therefore it pertains to the bishops to admit newly elected members into the Episcopal body by means of the sacrament of Orders.[12]

Priests, at their ordination, are signed with a special character and, as co-workers with the bishops, are able to act *in persona Christi capitis* (in the person of Christ the Head). It is in virtue of

10. *Lumen Gentium* 21, in *The Word on Fire Vatican II Collection: Constitutions*, ed. Matthew Levering (Park Ridge, IL: Word on Fire Institute, 2021), 74.

11. *Lumen Gentium* 21, in *Word on Fire Vatican II Collection*, 73.

12. *Lumen Gentium* 21, in *Word on Fire Vatican II Collection*, 74.

this anointing that priests are able to perform sacraments. Thus, as Bishop Barron explains, the priest is called to be a man of the sacraments. This is more than just being someone authorized to preside at religious functions, to stand up in front of the crowd and say certain appropriate things at Sunday services and at rites of passage like baptisms, weddings, and funerals. The priest is meant to be the one who, simply put, "makes things holy." Barron specifies that to be holy is to be a "friend of God."[13] Thus, the priest's work "as sanctifier will be to foster and cultivate a friendship between God and the people that [he serves]. [His] life will be about bringing people into intimacy with God."[14] Like Adam, who is considered the first priest by theologians in both the Jewish and Christian traditions, the priest must "walk with God" in easy fellowship. I was told many years ago as a seminarian by a good priest who served as my spiritual director that unless the parish priest is striving for holiness, the parishioners will not strive for holiness.

The priest is called to be that man in the midst of the Christian community who is the reconciler and the uniter of the Christian people with God and with each other, what St. Paul calls "ambassadors for Christ" (2 Cor. 5:20). In the first episode of his video series *Priest, Prophet, and King*, Bishop Barron explains that the word "adoration" comes from the Latin words *ad ora*, meaning "mouth to mouth." When the priest leads us before the Lord in adoration, it is a kind of "mouth-to-mouth" resuscitation in which the Lord breathes his life into us. That's how close we are called to be to the Lord in prayer! Likewise, the word "reconciliation" comes from the word

13. Barron, *Renewing Our Hope*, 55.

14. Barron, 55.

cilia, meaning "eyelash." Hence, when the priest brings us before the Lord for reconciliation, we come incredibly close—"eyelash to eyelash"—with God. That's how close each Christian is called to be to the Lord; and that's how close the priest is called to be to him, in order to lead his people to the Lord in right worship.

In his homily for the ordination of Dominican priests in 2019, Bishop Barron used the analogy of Jacob's ladder to describe the priest's role as mediator between heaven and earth. In Genesis, we find the remarkable story: "Jacob left Beer-sheba and went toward Haran. He came to a certain place and stayed there for the night, because the sun had set. Taking one of the stones of the place, he put it under his head and lay down in that place. And he dreamed that there was a ladder set up on the earth, the top of it reaching to heaven; and the angels of God were ascending and descending on it" (Gen. 28:10–12). Drawing upon the thought of St. Thomas Aquinas, Barron explains that the priest is called to be a bridge, a mediator, between God and human beings, and in so doing, "the priest participates in the very being of Jesus Christ, who is, in person, the bringing together of divinity and humanity."[15]

Understanding that the priest must be a man of service, a man who is in the world and yet not of the world, Bishop Barron reminds young priests to be careful not to exaggerate either extreme of Jacob's ladder. He emphasizes their need to balance both the transcendent end (the intellectual and spiritual dimensions) with the immanent end (the human and pastoral dimensions). The priest should have what Pope Francis famously described as "the smell of the sheep," and at the same time, he should be "comfortable in the company

15. Barron, 54.

of the angels."[16] The priest is meant to be a "pontifex" (literally, a "bridge-builder"), which is where we get the term "pontiff" from, as one who "makes of his own life a bridge between God and human beings."[17]

Another title applied cross-culturally to priests is "Father." A father "gives rise to another, but he also cherishes the other to whom he gives rise."[18] Priests are not bachelors—that is, men without ties who can come and go as we please, acting without responsibilities. No, we are men who have a family—the Church. We have children—those whom we are blessed to serve in our parishes and other apostolates. This is why we priests are called to be men of the sacraments: because this is precisely how we give life to our family—our parishioners. We as priests bring them from death to life in the sacrament of Baptism; we feed them with the Bread of Life, the Eucharist; when there is a rift in the family and our children need reconciliation, we offer them the sacrament of Penance; and when they are ill and need healing, we offer them the Anointing of the Sick.

BEING A PROPHET

The *munus* (office) of prophet is a particularly interesting one, to say the least. What is a prophet in the Old Testament? He is basically the permanent "nudge," the annoying one! The prophet is the one who speaks the divine truth. He is the one raised up by God to call Israel to recognize that God is God and that we are his creatures. As such, the prophets are always at odds with their community.

16. Barron, 55.

17. Barron, 55.

18. Robert Barron, *Light from Light: A Theological Reflection on the Nicene Creed* (Park Ridge, IL: Word on Fire Academic, 2021), 28.

They are always the peculiar ones, always slightly off—from Hosea's marriage to a prostitute, to Isaiah walking "naked and barefoot for three years as a sign" (Isa. 20:3), to the antics of Elijah, Jeremiah, Ezekiel, and so many others. With their lyrical speech and their unnerving word, they offer a "beauty that challenges the assumptions of the world."[19] These prophets were considered madmen by many in biblical times, yet they were the ones who got their writings into the Bible, not all of their critics!

The prophet invites, cajoles, and even shocks us with his words and actions. Thankfully, the prophetic call of the priest today rarely requires such dramatic gestures! But like those prophets, we must call the people to be transformed. This, too, was the key word of the preaching of John the Baptist and then of Jesus: *metanoiete* (Matt. 3:2 and 4:17). We are used to the translation "repent" for *metanoiete*, but Barron says that this frequent rendering is misleading: "This Greek term is based upon two words, *meta* (beyond) and *nous* (mind and spirit), and thus, in its most basic form, it means something like 'go beyond the mind that you have.' The English word 'repent' has a moralizing overtone, suggesting a change in behavior or actions, whereas Jesus' term seems to be hinting at a change at a far more fundamental level of one's being."[20] He further explains: "Jesus urges his listeners to change their way of knowing, their way of perceiving and grasping reality, their perspective, their mode of *seeing*."[21] Practically, this means: "Minds, eyes, ears, senses, perceptions—all

19. Robert Barron, "Episode 3: Challenging False Worship," *Priest, Prophet, King*, directed by Spirit Juice Studios (Skokie, IL: Word on Fire, 2014).

20. Barron, *And Now I See*, xiv.

21. Barron, xiv.

have to be opened up, turned around, revitalized. *Metanoia*, soul transformation, is Jesus' first recommendation."[22]

The task of the prophet is thus to call the world to a transformation of its way of seeing, and this transformation, of course, involves a turning away from a former, false view of things. We are not talking here about merely spiritual emotions or kind sentiments; we are talking about a worldview, which is why the office of the prophet is the one most closely tied to our intellectual life. In ancient Israel, the prophets called the people to be better neighbors to each other and especially the poorest—but more fundamentally, to turn away from the false gods and delusions around which they had ordered their lives to such devastating effect. Thus, the prophet's call for *metanoia* involves the negative task of confronting the world with its own profound disorder and delusion. Nevertheless, the goal of the prophet, in confronting the world with the truth, is to restore sight so that it can see what it is, and what—or *whom*—it was made for.

The *Baltimore Catechism* says that God created humankind "to show forth His goodness and to share with us His everlasting happiness in heaven."[23] And, bringing it back to basics, we must ask: What can we do to gain the happiness of heaven? The *Baltimore Catechism* tells us: "To gain the happiness of heaven we must know, love, and serve God in this world."[24] True friendship requires that both parties recognize the other for who they are and understand the true nature of the relationship that they share. The *Catechism of the Catholic Church,* quoting *Gaudium et Spes* 19, explains it this

22. Barron, xiv–xv.

23. *The New Saint Joseph Baltimore Catechism*, vol. 1 (Totowa, NJ: Catholic Book Publishing, 2012), 12.

24. *New Saint Joseph Baltimore Catechism*, 12.

way: "The dignity of man rests above all on the fact that he is called to communion with God. This invitation to converse with God is addressed to man as soon as he comes into being. . . . He cannot live fully according to truth unless he freely acknowledges that love and entrusts himself to his creator."[25]

In sum, friendship with God is the end goal of the prophet's stern call for *metanoia*—a new way of seeing that turns away from falsehood and idolatry and embraces the truth of our relationship to God—and is no different from Jesus' lovely assurance, "I came that they may have life, and have it abundantly" (John 10:10).

The true prophets of the Old Testament did not speak their own thoughts, however religious and lofty; they spoke the "word of the Lord." When Bishop Barron wishes to tell new priests about their prophetic role, he very simply calls them to be "men who speak the Word of God," and urges them, "Preach!" Yet he observes that our time does not simply need passionate preaching, but "intelligent and passionate preaching." Two things have to be held together, which Bishop Barron himself does so well: to be attentive to "the anxieties, expectations, and questions" of our day, while bringing to them "the illumination that comes from the Bible." A bad preacher either "offers answers to questions no one is asking" or "simply repeats and wallows in the questions."[26] Conversely, for a good preacher, "the authority of a real sermon comes not from the preacher—no matter how eloquent, intelligent, or spiritually insightful—but rather from the Holy Spirit."[27]

25. *Gaudium et Spes* 19, quoted in *Catechism of the Catholic Church* 27.

26. Barron, *Renewing Our Hope,* 56.

27. Robert Barron, *Proclaiming the Power of Christ* (Park Ridge, IL: Word on Fire Institute, [2008] 2021), xiv.

This prophetic vocation to preach the Word is not separate from the celebration of the sacrament of the altar. We need the prophets and their persistent call for genuine worship of the Lord in spirit and in truth. It is the role of the prophets in our midst to see the patterns of grace in our daily existence, and to bring us, the Israel of God, back from idolatry to right religion, from love of self to love of God and rightly ordered love of neighbor. The nature of our relationship to God is that of a creature to its Creator, and thus, friendship with God requires a recognition, on our part, of our creatureliness before God and all that it entails. This recognition of the true nature of our relationship to our God and Creator is nothing other than the virtue of religion, and thus it is clear that the virtue of religion is essential for friendship with God.

Priests serve this prophetic role as the custodians and practitioners of right worship. Day in and day out, priests' constant celebration of the sacraments throughout the world serves as a prophetic beacon, one that calls the world here and now to put aside the false gods and delusions that deform our lives and to enter anew into friendship with God by acknowledging the truth about who he is through the acts, words, and intentions of right worship. The consecration and elevation of the Host and the Chalice, the distribution of the Bread of Life to the people of God in fidelity to his words "Do this in remembrance of me"—these are the perfect prophetic gestures that Catholic priests will repeat until the end of time. Perhaps they are not as dramatic as Ezekiel lying on his side for 390 days, but they are timeless and effective (Ezek. 4:4–5).[28]

28. On the other hand, when St. Óscar Romero was martyred by gunfire in El Salvador while presiding over the Mass, the ritual became not only prophetic but also dramatic.

Priests are prophetic, then, not only by words directed at human beings today but by virtue of the acts of worship in which they lead the Church. In the Old Testament, the prophets seemed at times to be in conflict with the cultic priests. Over the course of Israel's history, there grew a separation between the priest, who officiated in temple sacrifices and in matters of interpretation of the Law, and the prophet, who was raised up charismatically by the Spirit of God. In the person of Christ Jesus, our "great high priest" (Heb. 4:14) in the New Covenant that he sealed in his own blood, the *munera* of prophet and priest are reconciled, for it is his Spirit that both filled the prophets of old and that has animated the Church and its apostolic leaders since the day of Pentecost (Acts 2). It is this Spirit that, by Christ's promise, fills the believer at Baptism. Priests and bishops receive a further gift of the Spirit that guides and fructifies their work: it makes the sacraments true sources of grace, gives power and life to the word of their teaching and preaching, and guides their leadership as they shepherd individual parishes and the Church as a whole.

BEING A KING

The final office of Christ in which priests share is that of kingship. But to understand how to share in Christ's kingship of the people of God, we have to first understand the kind of kingdom that he rules. In the prelude of *And Now I See*, tellingly titled "Change Your Way of Seeing," Barron draws our attention to the beginning of the Gospel of Mark. In Mark 1:15, the Lord Jesus arrives on the scene, having recently been baptized in the Jordan by John the Baptist, and emphatically states, "The time is fulfilled, and the kingdom of God has come near; repent, and believe in the good news." We might expect Jesus to give us a clear definition of this kingdom, but in fact, he never comes out in any of the Gospels with a direct statement of exactly what the kingdom of God is or is not. Jesus only defines the kingdom of God in parables. Notice that throughout the Gospels, he uses the following similes: like a treasure buried in a field; like a merchant searching for fine pearls; like a net thrown into the sea, which collects fish of every kind.

Why does Jesus never directly give us a definition of the kingdom of God? I suspect he doesn't do so, at least in part, because the kingdom of God is always more than we could ever ask for or imagine! Nevertheless, in a sense, the meaning of Jesus' message that "the kingdom of God has come near" is obvious enough: God's rule has broken in and is even now being established on earth. The kingdom of God, of course, is not any earthly dominion, but quite simply God's rule. But there is no sense in which God could ever have temporarily lost control over any part of his creation. So what new thing could have happened in first-century Palestine that would have warranted Christ's declaration that the kingdom of God was present as though it were breaking news (for indeed, Jesus presents his message as an *euangelion* or report of good *news*)? The obvious answer here is that Jesus himself was the news: in him, God's rule had become present on earth in a radically new way. Along similar lines, Bishop Barron explains,

> There have been libraries of books written on the subject of the "kingdom," some suggesting that it refers to a political realignment of Jewish society, others that it signals a purely spiritual condition beyond the world, still others that it points to a change of heart in the individual. To my mind, the metaphor of the

> kingdom, in its poetic richness, is legitimately open to all of those interpretations, but it has a primary referent in the person of Jesus himself. Jesus wants us to open our eyes and see him—more to the point, to see what God is doing in and through him. He himself is the kingdom of God coming into the world with transformative power.[29]

It appears, then, that when we ask the question "What is the kingdom?" we are using the wrong interrogative pronoun. Perhaps we should not ask "What?" but rather "Who?" is the kingdom of God. *It is Christ Jesus himself.* The central message that Jesus came to bring is the proclamation of the kingdom of God, and his good news is that the kingdom is present on earth, because, in him, the King is present, drawing the world in around him and establishing a new nation. But what do priests, or for that matter, ordinary Christians, have to do with this kingdom or with Christ's kingship? Furthermore, we should ask what has become of the kingdom of God in the time since the Ascension. Is the kingdom still here even though Christ no longer walks among us?

In anticipation of a point we will explore later in chapter 2, we must here observe that the Church is at once the seed of Christ's ingathering of all nations into the people of God and the ongoing mystical presence of Christ in the world. The Church is the "Mystical Body" of Christ, in which and through which our Lord's presence and rule lives on and extends into the world. Bishop Barron describes the Church as "an organism" whose members are the "eyes, ears, hands, feet, and heart" through which Jesus continues his work

29. Barron, *And Now I See*, xiii.

in the world.[30] And just as a person's presence is constituted by the presence of each cell and organ, similarly, Christ's presence, in virtue of which he proclaimed that "the kingdom is at hand," is constituted by the presence of each member of the Church, the Body of Christ. Each member of the Church thus mediates and radiates the presence and grace of Christ to the world, but just as the different organs and members of a body contribute in different ways to its presence and activity, so, too, the different members of the Church serve in different ways to mediate Christ's presence and kingship to the world. The bishops and priests govern the Church, moreover, in the way that the head governs the rest of the body, including its life-sustaining systems and organs.

Bishop Barron recalls St. Thomas' teaching that the role of the king is to be the one who helps to bring order to things.[31] The *munus* of kingship is seen, likewise, in the priest's work of ordering the charisms and life of the people of God. While the baptized "exercise certain types of leadership within the context of the Mystical Body," it is "ordained priests" who "assume the principal responsibility of ordering the charisms within the community toward the upbuilding of the kingdom of God."[32] However, the priest's role is certainly more than simply being the "organizer of the ministries of others," which Barron decries earlier. Indeed, the priest is also like a vital artery that carries the lifeblood of the body in his role as the celebrant

30. Robert Barron, *Letter to a Suffering Church: A Bishop Speaks on the Sexual Abuse Crisis* (Park Ridge, IL: Word on Fire, 2019), 71.

31. Thomas Aquinas, *De Regno*; see Barron, "Ordering the Kingdom," in *Priest, Prophet, King*.

32. Barron, *Renewing Our Hope*, 175. Here, Bishop Barron is commenting on Pope John Paul II's document *Pastores Dabo Vobis*, in which the pontiff refers to the priest as "head and shepherd of his people."

of the Eucharist. Barron emphasizes that "the Body and Blood of Jesus," which, by the consecration of the priest, are really present in the Eucharist, simply "*are* the Church, its lifeblood and raison d'être."[33] The priest is thus the medium through which Christ becomes physically present in the Church and in every participant in the Mass.

Again, the bishops and priests govern the Church, in part, as teachers who bear the sacred duty and anointing to guard and proclaim the Gospel and thereby to govern the faith and morals of the Church. As successors of the Apostles, the bishops and their priests receive the gift of the same Spirit that empowered the Apostles to proclaim the Gospel authoritatively both within the Church and to the whole world. Like the ancient kings, the role of the clergy is thus to unify the people of God, to teach its people authoritatively, and to lead them in right worship.

But it's important to notice certain ways in which Jesus transposes the ancient notion of kingship into a heavenly register. We've seen how the Old Testament, in its wisdom, is particularly suspicious of human kings. In our corrupt nature, kings all too easily succumb to the temptations of power and become tyrants. However, in Jesus—the ultimate model and exemplar for the priest—we observe an entirely new paradigm of kingship in which love, self-sacrifice, and humility replace so many of the vices that are characteristic of kings. In Jesus, the role of king resembles that of a shepherd. A true shepherd, as Jesus said, "lays down his life for the sheep" (John 10:11). Similarly, the Rite of Ordination of Priests enjoins the priest to pour out his life in the Lord's service. Remember, one of the basic

33. Robert Barron, *Eucharist* (Park Ridge, IL: Word on Fire Institute, [2008] 2021), 2.

messages of the Christian life, as articulated by Bishop Barron, is that it's not about us; it's about God and the service of God's people, just as Jesus' kingship is never about himself but for others. On the cross, his throne, he pours out blood and water from his wounded side, the fountain of the Church's sacramental life.

The very dignity of Christ's kingship is its radical humility, and as a representative of Christ, the priest must assume this mantle of pastoral humility. The kingly *munus* of the priest in a unique way especially requires the humility and wisdom to be open to the ideas of others. In many ways, for a priest to exercise his kingly *munus* requires that he be a listener! And not only to his fellow priests but to his people, especially those who are suffering.

CLERICALISM: A FAULTY UNDERSTANDING OF THE KINGLY *MUNUS*

Time and again throughout his papacy, Pope Francis has warned priests and bishops against clericalism. The priest is ordained to be a man of the sacraments and of service. When the priest, by his actions, inactions, or words, declares that he has come to be served, not to serve, he has lost sight of what Christ's kingship truly means. This kind of clericalism can be found in the saying, "The priest's hands are made for chalices, not for callouses." Yes, the priest's hands are made for chalices and for the dignified, right worship of God, but they are thereby also consecrated for service to the people of God. Ultimately, the priest is not made for worship of himself but for worship of God. The priest must always ask himself, "Do I try to draw the attention of the world back to the Creator of all things? Or do I, in my arrogance and pride, try to make my ministry all about me?" Pride is a very dangerous thing in the life of the priest.

Ambition is needed in anyone's life, including a priest's. But for what am I truly ambitious? If it's not the service of the kingdom of God, then my priorities need to be reordered!

When I was a young priest, I keenly remember feeling frustrated when my contemporaries were assigned to high-profile ministries. This one was a pastor, this other one was working in the chancery. What was I doing? Teaching in a high school! I felt underappreciated, forgotten, left out. Who knew who I even was anymore? Why wasn't I being asked to do these things that my peers were being asked to do?

I had to bring that to real prayer. Why was I so upset? What was at the root of my problem? Nothing less than my own fallen human nature. I let the focus slip away from Jesus and onto myself. I became the center of my own world, and the problems and worries that I permitted to so preoccupy me were really not meant to be the focus of my priesthood. Sure, I wasn't the pastor of a big parish, building so many new additions. I didn't get the then-coveted title of "Monsignor" when I reached the age of thirty-five.[34] But what I was doing as a priest, in fulfillment of the promise of obedience to my bishop and his successors that I took at my ordination, was what the Church needed me to do, and that was enough for me. If my bishop wanted me as a teacher for the spread of the Gospel message and, ultimately, for the kingdom of God, then I would learn to be a good one!

After all, it had been my own teachers in high school who had kindled my desire for the priesthood and for a spiritual life. How could I forget? As it happened, teaching became the focus of

34. My brother, trained by the Jesuits, urged me to join them and not become a diocesan priest! He said at my ordination, "If you are not the youngest Monsignor in Brooklyn soon, that's a sign you should have listened to me and become a Jesuit!"

my priestly life, although I have moved from teaching high school students to men in the seminary. For a time, I was academic dean of the North American College seminary in Rome, which does start to sound prestigious, but in reality, involved a whole lot of unglamorous administrative work. The pope's title "servant of the servants of God" also applies to those who work and teach at seminaries, because we are often equipping those fellow priests and religious who will themselves spend their time in pastoral ministry on the front lines. We have to remind ourselves and then teach others that, while we priests are in a sense chosen especially by God, his real favorites are the children, the poor, the sick, and the forgotten. If we listen to Christ, we will discover both the poverty and the grace of wherever we are called, however different it is from the life or priestly ministry we ever thought we would have.

BISHOP BARRON AS PROPHET, PRIEST, AND KING

When I read Bishop Barron or watch a video presentation by him, I am sure that this is not the life or the priestly ministry that he ever thought he would have. Did he ever think that he would become one of the twenty-first century's premier evangelists? God uses each of us, no matter who we are, exactly as he intends in this life. Priests are no different. No matter what ministry a priest may have in the Church, he is called to live out the triple *munera* of teaching, sanctifying, and governing.

Both in his work as a bishop within his diocese and as an evangelist in the public arena, Bishop Barron plays the roles of priest, prophet, and king. As bishop-priest, Barron celebrates the sacraments, including Holy Orders—the one sacrament that only bishops can perform. Moreover, his status as bishop-priest contributes to his prophetic role, both within the Church and in the world. Within the Church, his prophetic service takes the form of theological teaching in writing and homilies, and through his ministry, Word on Fire, his message has a global reach—both through the "old media," especially books, and the "new media," including the internet, social media, and video. When Barron engages in the public sphere in clerical regalia, his presence is a symbol of God's work of sanctifying the world. And in his engagement with the secular culture, he serves as a "prophetic beacon," drawing the world's attention back to the Creator of all things and away from the many falsehoods and idols to which it inclines. In the kingly role of his vocation as bishop, Barron is the father of his diocese, leading the governance and pastoral care of the people of God of the Diocese of Winona-Rochester, Minnesota.

One of his most important prophetic roles has been to address the great clerical scandals of the past thirty years. Bishop Barron's writings emphasize that the Church is the Mystical Body of Christ, the beautiful Bride of Christ, without stain or blemish (Eph. 5:27). Yet, at the same time, he is also forthright about the sinful nature of all who make up the Body of Christ, including Christ's ordained ministers—bishops, priests, and deacons. Christ is our Lord, and yet we all suffer from the *pusilla anima*, the fearful soul, which holds us back and drags us down.[35] Bishop Barron has not been deterred by the grave failures and crimes of his fellow priests and bishops, which have been laid out for all the world to see. He has taken this crisis very seriously, especially in his 2019 *Letter to a Suffering Church: A*

35. I will discuss this "small souledness" in comparison with "great souledness"—magnanimity—in chapter 3.

Bishop Speaks on the Sexual Abuse Crisis. In the next chapter, we will examine how the theology of the Church can guide us, especially priests, to remain hopeful and fall ever more deeply in love with Christ's Bride despite these grave scandals.

CHAPTER 2

Falling in Love with the Church, in Good Times and Bad: A Hopeful Ecclesiology

In the first chapter, I laid out what I hope is an inspiring vision of the Catholic priesthood in Jesus Christ through the words and example of Bishop Robert Barron. As I noted at the end, however, all is not well in the Church or the priesthood. Perhaps for today's young (and not-so-young) men entering the priesthood, the difficulties I will lay out in this chapter are now old hat. But for many Catholics—including Bishop Barron and myself—there has been a time of reckoning with the sins of the Church's ministers and hierarchy that has cast a dark shadow over the priesthood. Yet, as we will see, the nature of the Church herself gives us reasons for hope and for understanding how to be a priest amid these difficult times.

In his interview book, *To Light a Fire on the Earth*, Bishop Barron relates a story about how the perception of the priesthood changed during his lifetime, describing an interaction with his mother when he came home after completing his doctoral studies in Paris. John L. Allen Jr. writes:

> He recalled that she had a WELCOME HOME BOB! sign and some champagne on ice. After catching up for a while, he says, his mother mentioned that she had collected some news clippings for him on a table in his room.

"I go to my room, and there was this whole pile of sex abuse clippings," he says. "It was already happening in Chicago. I was unaware of that in Paris, I must say. I said, 'Wow, I know that guy,' and so on. Then my mom told me that, because of all that, when people asked about me she'd tell them that I was an author, not, in the first place, a priest. I remember thinking something has really shifted."[1]

Yes, in the past thirty years, the perception of the priesthood and—by extension, of the whole Catholic Church—has been altered, both from outside the Church and from within the Church itself. As someone who was in the seminary in the late 1990s, I can attest that we were made very aware of the problem of clerical sexual abuse. We were taught to be aware of the problem and to recognize any and all disordered tendencies within ourselves and within the community. However, nothing could have prepared a young priest for the onslaught of media coverage and scrutiny that 2002 brought to the Catholic Church in general and the priesthood in particular. It was a daily gauntlet to go and get the newspaper from the front of the rectory and see headline after headline in the New York tabloids, which proclaimed "Broken Vows" or, even more luridly, "Hot under the Collar." This was an age in which the internet was still, for

1. Robert Barron with John L. Allen Jr., *To Light a Fire on the Earth: Proclaiming the Gospel in a Secular Age* (New York: Image Books, 2017), 205.

most people, pretty much new, and required an investment of time ("dialing-up"). Twitter and Facebook hadn't even been invented yet! For most people, our news sources were primarily television and the print media.

After the enacting of the Dallas Charter for the protection of children and young people, and after more than a decade of its implementation, with much work and self-reflection and safeguarding, from my vantage point in Rome things seemed to be better in the Catholic Church back in the United States, even as I became academic dean at the North American College and defended my own doctorate in 2017.[2] But then came June 2018 with the revelations of the McCarrick scandal and its fallout. From Rome, I watched the abuse crisis show its global scope as the pope called bishops from across the world to discuss the problem.

Bishop Barron, reflecting on this situation in 2019, writes,

> It has been a diabolical masterpiece. I am talking about the scandal that has gripped the Catholic Church for the past thirty years and that continues to wreak havoc even today. When I was going through the seminary, it was fashionable to conceive of the devil as a symbol for the evil in the world, a sort of colorful literary device. But the storm of wickedness that has compromised the work of the Church in every way and that has left countless lives in ruins is just too ingenious to have been the

2. Bishop Barron discusses the Dallas protocols on pp. 81–85 of *Letter to a Suffering Church: A Bishop Speaks on the Sexual Abuse Crisis* (Park Ridge, IL: Word on Fire, 2019), and he is right to say "these institutional changes *have* made a substantial difference." The Catholic Church in the United States today has many effective procedures for safeguarding children that are even a model for other organizations.

> result of impersonal forces alone or merely human contrivance. It seems so thoroughly thought through, so comprehensively intentional. Certainly, in the ordinary run of history, bad things happen, but this scandal is just too exquisitely designed. It has corroded Catholic credibility so completely that the Church's work in evangelization, catechesis, preaching, outreach to the poor, recruitment of vocations, and education has been crippled. And most terribly, members of the Church, especially its most vulnerable, have been forced to live through a nightmare from which it seems impossible to wake. If the Church had a personal enemy—and indeed the devil is known as the enemy of the human race—it is hard to imagine that he could have come up with a better plan.[3]

AN AWARENESS OF THE CRISIS AND OF THE CALL

Yes, it has been a tough time to be a priest and a bishop in the Catholic Church, but, perhaps even more so, it has been a tough time to be a Catholic believer, a member of the lay faithful. As Bishop Barron predicts, "It will be mentioned in a thousand years when they say 'Crusades and witch hunts.' . . . They'll add, 'and the sex abuse scandal.' I'm convinced of that. I've said it's the worst crisis certainly in American Catholic Church history, and one of the worst in the whole history of the Church."[4] The Church has always acknowledged that there is the reality of sin and evil, that it affects the members of the Church, and that neither priests nor bishops

3. Barron, *Letter to a Suffering Church*, 3–4.

4. Barron with Allen Jr., *To Light a Fire*, 205.

nor even the pope are protected by God from sin (infallibility on doctrine does not mean impeccability in personal conduct!). As Bishop Barron observes, "The Church, from the very beginning and at every point in its development, has been marked to varying degrees by sin, scandal, stupidity, misbehavior, misfortune, and wickedness."[5] But perhaps never before has such a systematic failure of the Church's institutional life coincided with such a bright spotlight of external accountability. It's understandable that any sane member in an organization with such problems might ask whether it's worth staying.

Bishop Barron is obviously an intelligent, well-spoken man; if the Church were merely a human institution, perhaps he would be justified in leaving his fellow bishops behind and would find just as much public success on his own. But more importantly, he is a Catholic believer, one who knows that his Baptism and ordination root him in a reality much deeper than we can see. He writes that the Church is

> the Mystical Body of Christ, so we're not just a human institution, we're not just a coming together of like-minded people. We're a Mystical Body, and we're grounded in Jesus. We are cells and molecules in that body, and therefore in sacraments, in the liturgy, in the Eucharist, in the saints, in our great art, in our ethos and all that, we remain the Spotless Bride of Christ. Both those things are true, and we certainly can't deny the first, that there are people in the Church capable of great evil. I fully

5. Barron, *Letter to a Suffering Church*, 41.

> acknowledge it, and at times the Church has included all kinds of wicked people doing terrible things.[6]

If the Church isn't just the "coming together of like-minded people," then what is it? What brings unity to so many disparate people from every nation? The answer is in the name itself: our English "Church" is, in Greek, *ekklesia*, which refers to the convocation of a people. That term in turn stems from a Greek verb that literally means "called from." Thus, the word "Church" refers to an assembly of people who have been called together. This leads Barron to ask three questions: "Who does the calling? What is one being called from? And what is one being called to?"[7]

As to the first question, it is the Lord, "the sovereign voice of Christ," who is doing the calling.[8] Summoned by a "higher power,"[9] the Christian "relativizes his own will and places whatever desires he has within the context of the desire of a greater will."[10] Hence, the Christian has the attitude not of a prima donna, but of a hopeful child: "humble, alert to God's grace, waiting to be surprised."[11]

As to the second question, Barron says that the Christian has been "summoned out of what the Bible calls 'the world.'" I'm afraid that too often today people think that the Church calling us "out of the world" means that Christians aren't allowed to drink or just in

6. Barron with Allen Jr., *To Light a Fire*, 206.

7. Robert Barron, *Catholicism: A Journey to the Heart of the Faith* (New York: Image, 2011), 148.

8. Barron, 155.

9. Barron, 148. Bishop Barron is here speaking of St. Paul, a "supreme churchman," but it goes for all of us.

10. Barron, 148.

11. Barron, 148.

general have much fun at all. But Bishop Barron explains that the Bible means "the whole network of institutions, beliefs, behaviors, and practices that fosters division."[12] It is "a region of unlikeness" where our "similitude to God" is replaced by "what Augustine termed the *libido dominandi* (the lust to dominate)."[13] This world, Bishop Barron says, "is the realm of hatred, racism, sexism, violence, oppression, imperialism"—where might makes right.[14]

When we invite the wounded of the world into the confines of the Church, we are thus not setting up prison walls to pen them up far away from fun; we are instead offering them the protective walls of an ark, a "shelter from the storm, a boat tossing on the waves of a dysfunctional world."[15] Of course we know—through the abuse crisis in particular—that simply staying inside the visible Church does not always protect us from the *libido dominandi*, which is why we priests especially have to be vigilant shepherds, watching out for the good of the flock against wolves hiding in our own ranks. But ultimately, Bishop Barron warns, when we tell our people "what they are being called into," we should also be careful about extending the ark metaphor to every aspect of the Christian journey. For "the life of the Church is not meant to hunker down permanently behind the walls of a ship; it is meant to invade the world."[16] As Christians

12. Barron, 148–149.

13. Barron, 149.

14. Barron, 149. It must be said that the good thing about our world—as opposed to the Roman empire, for instance—is that many non-Christians recognize all these evils as evil. The problem is that, without grace, one usually ends up justifying one evil to fight another, such as when caring, enlightened people accept the destruction of the unborn as a path to a woman's well-being.

15. Barron, 150.

16. Barron, 151.

called out of the world and into God's life, we are then called to go back into the world to change it, not as self-sufficient lone rangers but precisely as the members of the community of Jesus, which bears the four marks of the Church: one, holy, catholic, and apostolic.

THE CHURCH IS ONE

Now that the internet is not quite so new as it was during the 2002 abuse crisis, not a week goes by without news of some disagreement or dissension among priests or even bishops. And that's not even taking into account what happens among the faithful in the comment boxes on those articles! It's hard to believe that Christians at any time in the past have had as many conflicting opinions as we do, if only because they just didn't have the free time. But when you read the history of the controversies over the great heresies or the Protestant Reformation, you realize that division has been a constant problem in the Church, even as far back as the churches founded by the Apostles.

Yet the Church is one, as Barron notes, because her founder is one. For all our diversity and apparent differences, Barron counters, "a Christian"—no matter what vocation or state of life that he or she finds himself or herself in—"is someone who, at the most fundamental level of his or her being, is centered on the one God of Jesus Christ."[17] This gift of the Holy Spirit in Baptism of course makes demands of us: that he and he alone be our area of "ultimate concern," to use the language of the Protestant theologian Paul Tillich. But even struggling, sinful Catholics can easily participate in the life of the Church's unity through some of her fundamental

17. Barron, 157.

elements. Barron highlights four: the creeds, the liturgy, the common commitment to service, and "our shared structure of order"—which is to say, the apostolic succession that includes priests and especially bishops.[18] Legitimate diversity in liturgical rites, spirituality, and schools of theology do not hurt this unity; they only enhance the fundamental point: we are not united because we all have the same backgrounds or prejudices or likes and dislikes. Barron comments that "the play between the one and the many in ecclesial life is like that which obtains within the tensive harmony of the three divine persons of God."[19]

This radical "Christocentrism" also applies to us struggling, sinful priests. It means that everything that we priests are is for and in Christ, which means everything we do and everything we say can be directed by Christ. Because of our ordinations, we priests are conformed ontologically—that is, in our very being—to Jesus Christ in a unique way (although rooted in the common priesthood of the baptized). Whether a priest is doing his laundry or celebrating Holy Mass, he is a priest; whether a priest is relaxing at home or hearing a confession, he is a priest. The downfall of so many priests has been the failure to realize that—no matter where we are and no matter what we are doing—we are always, in every situation and at all times, priests.

In many ways, people experience the sacrament of Holy Orders whenever they encounter an ordained minister of the Church—a deacon, priest, or bishop. That is why, in the introduction, I encouraged my fellow priests to wear their collars in public—not just to

18. Barron, 157.

19. Barron, 157.

make a statement of courage in the face of the world's rejection, but also for the priest himself, to remind himself what and who he is! The man people encounter is very human, with his own faults and failings, yet people expect something more. He needs to have the "smell of the sheep" on him, but he cannot wallow in the depths of sin himself. He needs to be also, as I will discuss more in chapter 3, a man who is also comfortable with the "company of angels" (see Rev. 5:11).[20]

When people encounter a priest (collar or no), they must meet a man for whom this ministry is not just a job; no, it is a vocation, a calling from God, a calling for service, a calling to conform one's life to the Lord in all aspects of his existence. "His mind, his will, his passions, his body, his private life, his public life, and his friendships must all belong to the Lord."[21] This does not mean he is a proud man who puts himself above others—not at all! Rather, it means that he will humbly recognize the "treasure" of being set apart for the Lord's service, even though he holds it in "earthen vessels" (2 Cor. 4:7 NABRE). He can't use the excuse of "trying to be normal" to justify laziness and sin! How many times have our people been unedified by priests who either intentionally or unintentionally cause scandal by imprudent language or humor, excesses against temperance, gluttony, and disordered affections?

True, when the people of God encounter a priest, they encounter a man, but at the same time, they encounter someone who for them represents the Church, Christ, and the divine. He is a visible sign of what they themselves are: "You shall be for me a priestly kingdom

20. Robert Barron, *Renewing Our Hope: Essays for the New Evangelization* (Washington, DC: The Catholic University of America Press, 2020), 55.

21. Barron, *Letter to a Suffering Church*, 90.

and a holy nation" (Exod. 19:6).[22] This can be a heavy burden to bear, but it is one that we must bear if we are to be chaste spouses and spiritual fathers to and for the Church. We do not need to bear it in isolation; we need to seek out and encourage priestly fraternity, not only to feel supported, but also to challenge one another. As Bishop Barron observes in his *Letter to a Suffering Church,* how much of our current crisis is because "many priests and bishops simply lacked the courage to engage in fraternal correction, especially if that meant losing a friend?"[23] Instead of this attitude, which is another form of clericalism, we have to point each other toward holiness.

In the end, while I can't make light of the burden of bearing God in a world often against him and his Church, the risk comes with a reward. First and foremost, Jesus promises us recompense in heaven if we are persecuted for righteousness and specifically for his name (Matt. 5:10–12). Indeed, in the Acts of the Apostles, this set the disciples' hearts rejoicing (Acts 5:41)! That should be reason enough, but so often there are even signs of that everlasting communion while on earth: people stopping you to say they are praying for you, to ask for a blessing, or to share some prayer request. How many times do I meet someone whom I've never met, but because of our common faith, there's an immediate experience of the Spirit who unites us in the Church? As Bishop Barron relates,

> The priesthood has taken me all over the world and deep into the hearts of people I've been privileged to serve. Some warned me long ago that I would be lonely as a priest, but I have never found

22. John Paul II, *Pastores Dabo Vobis* 13, apostolic exhortation, March 25, 1992, vatican.va.
23. Barron, *Letter to a Suffering Church*, 88–89.

> this to be true. On the contrary, the priesthood has connected me to an incredible number of people in a wide variety of contexts. My life as a priest of Jesus Christ has been unconventional, creative, energizing, unpredictable, and exciting.[24]

THE CHURCH IS HOLY

What does it mean for the Church to be "holy"? The revelations of 2002 and 2018 and every week on the internet have made this article of the creed a difficult one for many Catholics. The holiness of the Church, Barron points out, has the same root as its oneness: the Church is holy because Christ is holy, and the Church is the Mystical Body of Christ. He mentions that, in many languages, the word for health and wholeness is similar to the word for holy. Why? Because at its essence, "holiness is the integration that follows from placing God unambiguously at the center of one's concern; it is the coming together of all of one's faculties—mind, will, imagination, energy, body, sexuality—around the single organizing power of God. Or, to shift the metaphor, it is the suffusing of the entire self with the love of Christ."[25] And because she is holy, the Church's task is to make people holy.

In trying to understand how this holiness can coexist in the Church with the sin that we today cannot avoid acknowledging, Barron turns to history, to a key moment of theological reflection on this mystery: St. Augustine and his controversy with the Donatists. Augustine was a bishop in North Africa, then part of the Roman Empire, in a time after a Roman persecution had led many clergy to

24. Barron, "A Great Time to Be a Priest," Word on Fire, May 23, 2011, https://www.wordonfire.org/articles/barron/a-great-time-to-be-a-priest/.

25. Barron, *Catholicism*, 160–161.

hand over (*tradere* in Latin) the Scriptures as a way of repudiating the faith. The Donatists said these "hander-overs"—traitors—could not be forgiven, and they broke away from the universal (Catholic) Church to build their own church of the pure.

In his dispute with the Donatists, Augustine asked and answered questions that have reverberated long after the Donatists ceased to be. Are the sacraments offered by sinful ministers invalid? Can only sinless people serve a sinless Church? Augustine answered no to both of these questions. Barron writes, "Thank God Augustine held off this challenge, arguing that the grace of Christ can work even through entirely unworthy instruments. Otherwise, he saw, sin would overwhelm grace—and this would be repugnant to God's sovereignty."[26] The "efficaciousness" of the sacraments "is not a function of the minister's worthiness but of the grace of God gratuitously given," whether the priest turns out to be a despicable abuser or even just a garden-variety sinner. Bishop Barron comments,

> I cannot tell you how often during my thirty-three years of priesthood that I have been delighted to "hide behind the sacraments"! Long ago, I learned that these sacred signs and gestures, grounded in the life and ministry of Jesus himself, have far more power than any words of mine, no matter how clever or insightful.[27]

It is a great relief to us priests: holiness has its origin in the only one who is truly holy, God, and in particular God as Holy Spirit, the giver of life breathed on the Apostles by Christ and poured out on

26. Barron, 163.

27. Barron, *Renewing Our Hope*, 56. The phrase "hide behind the sacraments" was used as "gentle teasing" by Protestant ministers to the sick who were observing how much easier the task could be for a Catholic priest.

the whole Church at Pentecost. Bishop Barron observes, "It is this same Holy Spirit who, throughout the history of the Church to the present moment, gives vitality and energy to the Mystical Body."[28] Even though we, his people, and in particular his ministers, are sinful, flawed human beings, graces flow through us to one another and the whole human race.

For Barron, in order to see the holiness of the Church more tangibly, we need the great communion of saints. Throughout his writings, Bishop Barron has urged his readers and listeners to turn to the example and intercessions of the holy ones of God,[29] observing, "The Church is most beautiful in her saints."[30] Barron describes them as "those who have allowed Jesus to get into their boats and who have thereby become not superhuman or angelic but fully human, as alive as God intended them to be."[31] The saint is one who, simply put, has God and God alone as his or her center of ultimate concern.

The world, as I said above, thinks that to follow God makes one drab and boring. Billy Joel sang about preferring the laughter of sinners to the sorrows of the saints. But as Bishop Barron relates the stories of these "pivotal players" of Catholicism, we realize that, despite their travails and suffering, real saints are anything but drab and boring![32] Although they are drawing from the same

28. Barron, *Letter to a Suffering Church*, 71.

29. See, in particular, Barron, "A Vast Company of Witnesses: The Communion of Saints," in *Catholicism*, 195–223.

30. Barron, *Renewing Our Hope*, 25.

31. Barron, *Catholicism*, 196.

32. Bishop Barron's book *The Pivotal Players* includes seven canonized saints, but he also remarks that a number of female saints in particular—"Teresa of Avila, Bernadette of Lourdes, Edith Stein, Mother Katharine Drexel, Thérèse of Lisieux, Mother Teresa of Kolkata," and "Mary, the Mother of God"—could also have been chosen as "pivotal players" but had already been included in *Catholicism*. See *Pivotal Players: 12 Heroes Who Shaped the Church and Changed the World* (Park Ridge, IL: Word on Fire, 2020), ix.

divine source, the saints are fascinatingly diverse. Barron describes sanctity thus: "The holiness of God is like a white light: pure, simple, complete. But when that light shines, as it were, through the prisms of individual human lives, it breaks into an infinite variety of colors," and he reminds us beautifully that "the Church revels in the variety of its saints because it needs such diversity in order to represent, with even relative adequacy, the infinite intensity of God's goodness."[33]

The radical poverty and freedom of St. Francis; the balanced brilliance of St. Thomas Aquinas; the fiery mysticism of St. Catherine of Siena; the brilliant erudition of St. John Henry Newman; the spiritual intensity and simplicity of St. Thérèse of Lisieux—these are not simply people commended by the Church for following the rules well; they are people whose lives we find endlessly fascinating. Even those who have no faith take interest in such Catholics, because they show the glory of God through a human being fully alive. And these famous names are only the tip of the iceberg; the Church recognizes saints from so many continents, races, and social classes—all of whose stories nevertheless share in one story: the struggle and the glory of embracing the cross and following the way of the Lord. By looking to them, we can see the beauty of Christ's Bride by glimpsing a foretaste of the heavenly glory that awaits us if we suffer with him (see Rom. 8:17). Bishop Barron reminds us to turn off our cable news networks and look up from our gloomy social media feeds for a while and open a book—or listen to a talk or watch a documentary—and to receive the Gospel anew through recalling the lives of those in whom the Holy Spirit's invisible work has become visible on earth.[34]

33. Barron, *Catholicism*, 223.

34. A saint is someone in whom God has "shown a profit," according to Flannery O'Connor. Flannery O'Connor, *The Habit of Being* (New York: Farrar, Strauss, and Giroux, 1979), 307.

Therefore, we contemporary Christians—priests especially—do not need to fear the great call to holiness! Christ will not lead us into a "beige" realm of dull conformity, but rather, as Bishop Barron assures us, down "the strangest, most exotic, surprising, and uncanny of all of the religious paths."[35] We as priests must strive to be holy, to be exemplars for the people with whose care we are charged. As a wise spiritual director once told me, "Don't aim for purgatory! If you miss, you go to a lot hotter place!" As priests, we must ourselves aim for heaven. And by our actions and attitudes, we must help lead our people to rely on the Lord who alone can bring them to heaven.

THE CHURCH IS CATHOLIC

One of the brightest stars in the Church's constellation of saints is Augustine, whose work still engages seekers and scholars alike. As I discussed above, Augustine was no stranger to this struggle to appreciate both the holiness and sinlessness of the Church, nor to the arguments that the sinfulness of the Church's members invalidated her status as the one true Church. When Augustine was arguing with the Donatists in the fourth century about which church was the true one, he could already appeal to the fact that the "Catholic Church" was spread throughout time and place—and how much more can we do so today!

But "catholicity," of course, refers to more than this empirical spread of the faith. The name "catholic" means "universal." Even here, we can observe that not all Christians maintain communion with the Catholic Church, nor has the Church yet evangelized *every* people and land, at least not as well as we would like. But

35. Barron, *The Strangest Way: Walking the Christian Path* (Park Ridge, IL: Word on Fire Institute, [2002] 2021), 3.

nevertheless, Barron notes, the Church demonstrates both "internal integrity" and "universal outreach."[36] That is why, while acknowledging that Christians of other churches and ecclesial communities are part of the body of Christ through Baptism, the Second Vatican Council still insisted that the Church of Jesus Christ "subsists in" the Catholic Church.[37] In Barron's words, "The Catholic Church has all of the gifts that Christ wants his people to have: Scripture, liturgy, theological tradition, sacraments, the Eucharist, Mary and the saints, apostolic succession, and papal authority. From the Roman Catholic point of view, all of the non-Catholic Christian churches have sacrificed one or more of these qualities and therefore fall short of completeness or catholicity."[38] Barron explains that "because that communion possesses full integrity . . . it operates 'according to the whole.' A wise teacher of mine once commented on the 'grandma's attic' quality of Catholicism, by which he meant our wonderfully stubborn refusal ever to throw anything out."[39]

According to Barron, the Church demonstrates her catholicity when she embraces a "culture and language transcending universality."[40] People today often argue that this means that Catholicism tries to be a one-size-fits-all solution to the religious and spiritual needs of people everywhere, and a system imposing Western culture on non-Western cultures (indigenous, African, Asian, etc.). How can we avoid this charge of intolerance while saying that the Church is

36. Barron, *Catholicism*, 164.

37. *Lumen Gentium* 8, in *The Word on Fire Vatican II Collection: Constitutions*, ed. Matthew Levering (Park Ridge, IL: Word on Fire Institute, 2021), 53.

38. Barron, *Catholicism*, 164.

39. Barron, 164–165.

40. Barron, 165.

the universal sacrament of salvation (*Lumen Gentium* 48) and that Jesus Christ is the sole source of salvation? Barron answers,

> The best way to respond to such concerns is to show how the many faiths, religions, and philosophies do, in fact, to varying degrees, already participate in the fullness of Christ's gifts and are hence implicitly related to the Catholic Church. We have already gestured toward the significant points of contact with other Christian faiths, but there are many analogies with the non-Christian religions as well. With Jews, Catholics share a belief in the one Creator God who called Israel to be a light to the world. With Muslims, Catholics hold to the faith in the one providential God of mercy who speaks through a variety of prophets. Buddhists and Catholics come together in a keen sense of the finally ineffable quality of ultimate reality, and in their commitment to definite forms of mystical contemplation. Catholics and Hindus share a profound sense of the immanence of God to the world. All of these points of contact, all of these "rays of light" are not only *semina verbi* (seeds of the word) but also *semina catholicitatis* (seeds of catholicity).[41]

The individual priest is meant to be parochial in one sense—that is, to order his life around the care of the parish that is entrusted to him or whatever his assignment may be, whether a chaplaincy, an educational assignment, or something else that is asked of him by his bishop or legitimate ecclesiastical superior. He should not get distracted from his own particular task by worrying too much about

41. Barron, 166.

the whole world. Even Jesus, the Savior of the world, focused in his earthly ministry on "the lost sheep of the house of Israel" (Matt. 15:24). At the same time, the priest is not meant to be parochial in the pejorative sense of that word, meaning narrow or limited in scope or perspective. The priest is meant to realize the great diversity that is the Church, as the living, breathing Body of Christ. How can he do this? Allow me to suggest two simple ways.

First, he can realize that worship and spirituality can look different in diverse communities. For instance, we know the Catholic Church exists in both the Eastern churches and in the Latin Church. How much do we as Roman Catholic priests know about the Ruthenian Catholic Church or the Maronite Catholic Church, which are in union with Rome and as Catholic as any Roman Catholic? How much do we know about the Personal Ordinariates created to welcome former Anglicans into the Catholic Church and who pray with *Divine Worship: The Missal*, which is based on the Book of Common Prayer? These believers are in union with the pope and are as Catholic as Latin Rite Catholics—even the former Anglican priests who, by a special dispensation, have been ordained Catholic priests while married. How much are we willing to welcome those Catholics who wish to attend Holy Mass in the Extraordinary Form—a.k.a., the Traditional Latin Mass? On the other hand, are we uncomfortable with the traditions of the Black Catholic Church and the reverent inclusion of gospel music in the Latin liturgy?

Second, he can be open to the various spiritualities and ecclesial movements that exist in the Church that have the full approval and support of the Church. In answering the question of how the Church will overcome its current crises, Bishop Barron proposes that institutional reforms or personal piety—however necessary—are not enough. The great crises of the past were answered by great spiritual movements, such as the Benedictines, Franciscans, and Jesuits. So "who can fail to appreciate that this is precisely the time for new orders, new movements, new works of the Spirit!"[42] Perhaps the priest may not pray as part of the Charismatic Renewal, but is he willing to permit and support such a group in his parish? Is he willing to permit ecclesial movements that function with the complete support of Rome to flourish in his parochial community, even if it is not his particular sense of Church, whether it be the Focolare Movement, Communion and Liberation, or the Neocatechumenal Way?[43]

In terms of the popular devotion of the people to whom he is assigned, is the priest willing to learn about the devotion that a particular parish may have toward the Divine Mercy, Padre Pio, Thérèse of Lisieux, or some other saint or servant of God that might be popular in the parish but not with the priest himself? Will he be willing to learn about the popular devotions that mean so much to his people?

Is the priest a man of welcome to people of all languages and cultures? Is he willing to at least be welcoming to Spanish-language speakers, which are the growing majority of Catholics in the United States, if not to learn the Spanish language himself?[44] Is he willing to learn at least some of the cultural traditions of the people who are his parishioners, even if he does not himself know the language?

42. Barron, *Letter to a Suffering Church*, 96.

43. None of this is to say that a priest should turn a blind eye to potential abuses in new communities, but rather that he should cooperate with his bishop and the Vatican in making fair and open-minded judgments rather than being jealous of others' success.

44. See Michael Kueber, *Preaching to Latinos: Welcoming the Hispanic Moment in the U.S. Church* (Washington, DC: The Catholic University of America Press, 2022).

Here I am thinking about some of the great cultural traditions from various Latino countries, Italy, Vietnam, or the Philippines—but in the US Church, there are so many more. All of this is part of being the welcoming and loving face of Christ that every priest is called to be, even if he is never sent as a missionary to Africa or Asia. Were the Americas themselves not "the ends of the earth" not so long ago?

We can never prepare in seminary for every unique culture and person that we will encounter in our ministry, but we can prepare to have an attitude of gratitude for each legitimate difference that we meet in our people. Just as the diversity of canonized saints shows us the incredible breadth of God's generosity and faithfulness, so the piety of the faithful in all of its varieties brings out different forms of beauty latent in Christ and his Gospel. Far from being annoyed or frightened by these differences, we can come to see them as the manifestations of the personality of the Bride of Christ with whom we have fallen in love.

THE CHURCH IS APOSTOLIC

Ultimately, the Church fearlessly brings the Gospel to "all nations" (Matt. 28:19), even "to the end of the earth" (Acts 1:8), because we were commanded to do so by Jesus. But when I say that Jesus gave this commission "to us," I am assuming the last mark of the Church: that of being apostolic. It was to the Apostles that Christ said these things, but our Church is founded on the Apostles. This is a fact that particularly hits home for me when I look at the chalice that I have from my own priestly ordination. The chalice of a priest is a unique, personal thing; in a way, it reflects the ministry of the priest. When I was ordained, I was given a chalice that had been used by another priest for close to fifty years; he had been given it by his pastor, who, as it turns out, was my great-uncle. When I use that chalice at Mass, I think back to the thousands of Masses offered using that chalice and paten by these two priests and myself in the course of our lifetimes. That chalice is, for me, a symbol of apostolicity; to carry on this most sacred tradition has been the privilege and duty of the Lord's ministers going back to the beginning. In his First Letter to the Corinthians, St. Paul writes: "For I received from the Lord what I also handed on to you, that the Lord Jesus on the night when he was betrayed took a loaf of bread, and when he had given thanks, he broke it and said, 'This is my body that is for you. Do this in remembrance of me'" (1 Cor. 11:23–24).

It is not only through the successor of Peter (see Matt. 16:18) that we continue the ministry of the Apostles; every bishop carries on the apostolic mandate. Barron reminds us of this beautifully: "When I was ordained a priest, a successor of the Apostles laid hands on me and thus gave me a share in his authority. Whatever capacity I have to govern, sanctify, or teach in the church comes from my participation in that apostolic charism."[45] A priest by his ordination is intrinsically tied to his bishop. In fact, one of the three ordination promises taken by a man who presents himself for the sacrament of Holy Orders is that of respect for and obedience to his ordinary, meaning his bishop and his bishop's successors.

I have warned seminarians over my years as a seminary formator against joining a diocese because they happen to like the current bishop due to his ecclesiological or liturgical stance. At the risk of sounding cruel or cynical, diocesan bishops have a habit of either being transferred to another diocese, dying, or retiring! If a priest's

45. Barron, *Catholicism*, 168.

whole connection to a diocese is through the human personality of the departed bishop, what does he do when the new bishop is appointed—perhaps one with whom he does not necessarily agree or even personally like? What does one do when even a pope comes along whose style, personality, or decisions are not liked or appreciated by a particular priest?

Well, as I tell the seminarians whom I am blessed to form, they must remember that through the bishop they find their link to the apostolic succession, to the mandate of Christ. Just as the bread and wine become the Body and Blood of Christ not through the merits of the minister but through the power of Holy Orders, so the Church is still governed by Christ through the power of Holy Orders (as I'll discuss more in chapter 3). This doesn't mean they have to believe that every action of their ecclesiastical superiors is the right one! But it does mean that they must respect and obey their bishop and the Holy Father, the pope. Unless what is being asked of them will mean disobeying natural law, moral law, ecclesiastical law, or civil law—that is, unless one's conscience, which is a fully informed Catholic conscience, is violated—a priest must always respect and obey his bishop and respect the teachings of the Holy Father.

This requires a great deal of humility on the part of the priest. It requires that the priest always work under the hermeneutic of trust, rather than that of suspicion. The Church is our Mother: she nourishes, guides, and supports us on this journey of life, just as our natural mother does. We must trust her and her judgments—which is to say, ultimately, we have to trust the Lord. When, on the other hand, laws are being broken—particularly involving the abuse of the vulnerable—the priest needs not only to follow the procedures of the Church to address these problems, but also to heed our Lord in Matthew 18:15–17 and only turn to public denunciation when other avenues of redress are failing.

A HOPEFUL ECCLESIOLOGY

Yes, we acknowledge that there are problems in the Church. No one will be more aware of that than a priest with open eyes and ears. It is he who sees the wounds on the Body of Christ up close, even those wounds that are inflicted by himself and his brother clerics. It is he who sees that the Church, as the Mystical Body of Christ, is sinless, but we who make up the Church and make daily decisions in her offices are sinners. He sees her as a collection of people who are broken, bloodied, bruised, and battered, and yet who still join together, reborn from the dead in the sacraments of Baptism and Reconciliation, united in the sacrament of Christ's true Body and Blood, the Eucharist, and made into the beautiful Bride of Christ.

Once again, the priest is no bachelor; he is not a man who is unattached and who can come and go as he pleases. As we will discuss in the next chapter, his celibacy is the sign of a commitment, one made until death to Christ's Bride, the Church. In many ways, what is needed today for priests is the gift of perseverance. As the bishop says to the candidate for Holy Orders at his installation to the ministry, "May God who has begun the good work in you bring it to fulfillment" (see Phil. 1:6). God has truly begun good work in the life of every cleric! The key is not to lose sight of the reason for our hope—the sure and certain truth that Jesus Christ is Lord! And that hope is lived in a Church that is one, holy, catholic, and apostolic; a Church that is both the Bride of Christ and the Mystical Body of Christ; a Church to which Bishop Barron and so many other clerics have been wed.

The priest is thus called to be a realist in the deepest sense. He is called to see the grim facts on the ground but also the deeper and more encouraging realities, such as the ontological change in himself and others, and the ever-verdant Spirit of God. As Bishop Barron observes, "The Church calls people to be not spiritual mediocrities, but great saints, and this is why its moral ideals are so stringent. Yet the Church also mediates the infinite mercy of God to those who fail to live up to that ideal (which means practically everyone). This is why its forgiveness is so generous and so absolute."[46] Just as any good husband knows that, on the human level, his wife is not perfect, but still loves her and has pledged to be true to her "in good times and in bad," the good priest sees the sin, the corruption, the scandal, but—if he also allows himself to be filled with Christ's love for his Bride—he will not abandon her. He will instead give himself up for her (see Eph. 5:25) and, by his own self-sacrifice—his prayers, works, and spiritual offerings—love her even more. The priest sees the wounded Body of Christ, and he knows it is his task to help Christ heal her.

46. Robert Barron, *Vibrant Paradoxes: The Both/And of Catholicism* (Park Ridge, IL: Word on Fire, 2016), 7.

CHAPTER 3

Heroic Priesthood: Priest as Mystagogue and Doctor of the Soul

Movies today are full of superheroes, and the most compelling of these are previously ordinary men or women who find themselves with amazing abilities, whether through their own ingenuity (Batman, Iron Man), some fortunate accident (Spider-Man, Captain Marvel), or some kind of attempt to create a supersoldier (Captain America). This image of "building a superhero" comes to mind when looking at the title of Robert Barron's December 1997 interview in *U.S. Catholic* entitled "How to Build a Better Priest."[1] This was the first time I had ever encountered then-Fr. Barron, and I was galvanized by what he wrote. When he began the interview saying, "For too long we've had a preferential option for mediocrity in the priesthood,"[2] I was ready to applaud. He freely admitted that the

1. "How to Build a Better Priest: The Editors Interview Father Robert Barron," *U.S. Catholic* 62, no. 12 (December 1997): 10–16.

2. "How to Build a Better Priest," 10.

priesthood was in crisis. For him, this crisis facing our time had everything to do with our vague and deflated conception of priestly identity. Speaking of his own seminary experience, Barron remarked,

> If you asked my classmates . . . "Tell me what a priest is," you'd probably hear, "Um . . . We don't have the words for that." Our problem is not clericalism—it's the inability to say and celebrate who priests are. We become apologetic, self-conscious. We're worried that if we celebrate priesthood, we'll offend this group or that group. Along the way we forget to ask, "Who on earth would be attracted to this, when we can't even say who we are? Who would find this rich and compelling?"[3]

Elsewhere, he makes a similar observation:

> As many commentators have pointed out, there is a sort of crisis in confidence and identity among priests today. Many new ministries and roles of service have emerged in the Church, and lay people are assuming, legitimately, many of the tasks formerly performed exclusively by the clergy. This phenomenon has led some priests to wonder what their unique contribution might be, what they, distinctively, can offer to the people of God.[4]

And this was before the scandals of 2002 and thereafter! With this crisis of ambivalence about the priesthood in mind, we need to ask

3. "How to Build a Better Priest," 15.

4. Robert Barron, *Bridging the Great Divide: Musings of a Post-Liberal, Post-Conservative Evangelical Catholic* (Lanham, MD: Rowman & Littlefield, 2004), 235.

ourselves some questions: What is a priest? What does he do? And what sort of man are we looking for in the priesthood today?

This much-discussed quest for a priestly identity reflects a fairly contemporary problem. In prior generations, it was commonly understood and accepted that the priest was *alter Christus* (another Christ) and that it was his role to live out the *munera* (offices or duties) of teaching, administrating, and sanctifying, as I discussed in chapter 1. Moreover, this "other Christ" was rarely a lone minister; rather, he could grow into his role in close collaboration with other priests. To use my home parish in Brooklyn as an example, in 1955, the parish complex was a New York city block, which housed the church, the rectory, the convent, the brothers' house, the boys' school, and the girls' school. The pastor of the parish was an auxiliary bishop, assisted by the senior curate (who had been ordained around twenty-five years prior) and two or three other curates (including one who was newly ordained). Also present in the rectory were a few other priests who were assigned full-time to other ministries but assisted in the parish. By the time I was growing up, things were slightly different, but there was still a larger, coeducational grade school with a few religious sisters and brothers teaching in it, and a rectory that housed a pastor and three full-time priests. Today, the parish is staffed by one priest—the pastor—and the grade school, employing no religious at all, is a Catholic academy shared with a neighboring parish. Moreover, that pastor's authority and good name can be challenged in ways unimaginable in the days of my grandparents or even my parents.

In the context of the now radically diminished institutional importance of the local parish, it is no longer possible simply to learn how to be a priest by example or osmosis. From the perspective of worldly honor, there seems to be little about the role of the parish priest today that would generate interest in, or enthusiasm about, the priesthood. Priests today are overburdened by the weight of parochial administration and hampered in their role by the priesthood's general loss of credibility due to the grievous sins of some clerics, including even eminent cardinals and bishops. Some of my brother priests in the United States have told me that they no longer feel comfortable traveling in clerical garb or religious habit due to the looks that they receive; many others avoid wearing them anywhere off parish property for the same reason.[5]

And yet, I contend that there is no better time to be a Catholic priest. Seminary formation today is certainly more uniform and better than it was in the 1980s and 1990s—primarily due to an embrace, an understanding, and an implementation of Pope St. John Paul II's post-synodal exhortation *Pastores Dabo Vobis* (1992), the United States Conference of Catholic Bishops' *Program of Priestly Formation in the United States*,[6] and the Congregation for the Clergy's 2016 instruction entitled *The Gift of the Priestly Vocation* (*Ratio Fundamentalis Institutionis Sacerdotalis*).[7] By and large, there seems to be much more of a unity of mind and heart in what the Church is looking for in her priests and in priestly formation today.

5. As I've explained earlier in this book, I think we have good reason to overcome this discomfort and wear our priestly identity on our sleeve, as it were—but I understand the feeling.

6. See *Program of Priestly Formation in the United States of America*, 6th ed. (Washington, DC: United States Conference of Catholic Bishops, 2022).

7. Congregation for the Clergy, *The Gift of the Priestly Vocation* (*Ratio Fundamentalis Institutionis Sacerdotalis*) (Vatican City: L'Osservatore Romano, 2016), http://www.clerus.va/content/dam/clerus/Ratio%20Fundamentalis/The%20Gift%20of%20the%20Priestly%20Vocation.pdf. The Congregation for the Clergy has been renamed the "Dicastery for the Clergy" since this document was published.

Moreover, priests are more necessary than ever for the sanctifying of the world. In the absence of the old popular esteem and social support given to the clergy, what is necessary today for the priest is a radical reconfiguration to the person to whom he was configured at his ordination—Jesus Christ, the Lord, the one, true high priest. As Pope St. John Paul II said,

> To be a true help to young people and to all the lay people involved in the mission, and to live fully our own priesthood, it is essential always *to put Jesus Christ at the center of all our efforts.* St. Cyprian rightly said that the Christian, every Christian, is "another Christ"—*Christianus alter Christus.* But we would be even more correct to say, with the whole of our great tradition, *Sacerdos alter Christus* [the priest is another Christ]. This too is the deepest meaning of his vocation to the priesthood and of the joy felt by every new priest who is ordained.[8]

But what would it look like if, despite all the challenges that they face, priests embraced the full grandeur and gravity of their office as *alter Christus* with the joy and enthusiasm that belongs to it? Bishop Barron offers suggestions that are both challenging and inspiring for priests, seminarians, and those discerning a vocation. Properly understood, the vocation of a priest is as soul doctor and mystagogue, imparting and exemplifying the radical vision of Christian life, serving and inspiring Christ's flock. This is a great and high calling and should be celebrated as such. Priests, while serving their flock in

8. John Paul II, "Address of Pope John Paul II to the Clergy of Rome," February 13, 1997, vatican.va.

humility and with full consciousness of their own sins and those of their fellow clergy, should never forget the tremendous importance and dignity of their office. We should embrace the call to be heroic and the one who gives us the power to achieve it.

BUILDING A BETTER PRIEST

Don't all priests appreciate this dignity of their office? In a word, no. In his *U.S. Catholic* interview, Bishop Barron went on to identify as a source of this mediocrity a model of priesthood in which the priest is understood primarily as an "organizer of ministries."[9] I was all too familiar with this model and with the bland, managerial priest that it yields. I knew that the "ministry organizer" priest was no caricature, moreover, and had heard this description asserted without irony at a seminary where many of my diocesan brothers studied at the time.

Instead, Barron proposed that the priest should be "someone of great soul. Someone who is magnanimous in the literal sense: *magna anima*, having a big soul. Someone who is in touch with human compassion, with love, with justice. Someone in touch with that deepest part of himself and others, and who lives and breathes the great culture that feeds the soul."[10] In his book *And Now I See*, Barron contrasts this great soul with the "*pusilla anima* (the small soul)," which leads us to "live in a very narrow space, in the *angustiae* (straits) between this fear and that, between this attachment and that."[11] I have recognized this *pusilla anima* in myself, time and again: the desire, even as a priest, to cling to the things of this world,

9. "How to Build a Better Priest," 10.

10. "How to Build a Better Priest," 13.

11. Robert Barron, *And Now I See: A Theology of Transformation* (Park Ridge, IL: Word on Fire Academic, [1998] 2021), xv.

with its comforts and honors, its disordered affections and sin. But I also recognize that the vocation of the priesthood is greater.

We trace this notion of magnanimity back to Greek philosophy. According to Aristotle, the magnanimous man is someone concerned above all about not selling short his own greatness.[12] As priests, however, we don't look to our own excellence; instead, we recognize ourselves to be unworthy but chosen ministers of Christ, whose life we share and seek to communicate. It is his call that we should never sell short. We can overcome our fears and attachments "when we surrender in trust to the bearing power of God." For then "our souls become great, roomy, expansive. We realize that we are connected to all things and to the creative energy of the whole cosmos."[13] In order to open ourselves to this great calling, we must embody our trust in God over our fear and self-protection. This requires, Barron says, "a commitment at the level of your behavior, your lifestyle,"[14] adding, "it can't just be a disembodied intellectual exercise."[15] In the interview, he identifies two areas of this concrete commitment of trust over fear: celibacy and simplicity.

To many modern people, the ability to live celibacy joyfully must seem like a superpower on par with leaping tall buildings or stopping speeding bullets; it is so completely against our culture's understanding of sexual love as an irrepressible need. In "How to Build a Better Priest" (and a related article entitled "The Priest as Bearer of the Mystery"), Bishop Barron cautioned against countering this cultural bias with arguments based primarily in

12. Aristotle, *Nicomachean Ethics* 4.3.3.

13. Barron, *And Now I See*, xv–xvi.

14. "How to Build a Better Priest," 15.

15. "How to Build a Better Priest," 15.

"practical or even 'pastoral' considerations,"[16] such as the difficulties of the Church supporting a priest's family or maximizing the time available for ministry. Instead, he proposed framing it as "a kind of irrational, over-the-top, poetic, symbolic expression of the soul in love," the kind of "strange" even "excessive" choice made by "people in love."[17] He compares it to the woman who broke open a jar of perfume on Jesus' feet in the Gospels; it would be unreasonable were it not true that this sacrificial act manifests her "ultimate concern."[18] Hence, "the celibate [priest] is someone who, in the strangeness of his choice of lifestyle, reminds the people of God of their most profound destiny"—"that power which is ever-greater than [we] can think, feel, or imagine."[19] This is to live celibacy not primarily as a sacrifice or restraint but as a spiritual or supernatural gift.

He also calls us to attend to "all that language about poverty and asceticism that the spiritual teachers insist upon."[20] While a vow of poverty is not required of every kind of priest, it is necessary to seek an appropriate level of simplicity for one's own vocation, in part by keeping in mind the greater poverty lived by so many saints. In recalling the great evangelists in the Church's history, Bishop Barron points particularly to St. Anthony of the Desert and St. Benedict, as their "embrace of poverty, simplicity, care for the poor, and trust in God's providence galvanized the imagination of people in the late

16. Barron, *Bridging the Great Divide*, 232.

17. "How to Build a Better Priest," 15.

18. Barron, *Bridging the Great Divide*, 233. The language of "ultimate concern" is from the Protestant theologian Paul Tillich, from whom Bishop Barron gleans an interpretation of this scriptural story as showing the reasonability of an "unreasonable" gesture of love.

19. Barron, 233.

20. "How to Build a Better Priest," 15.

Roman period."[21] Their example of simplicity can and should be renewed in every age by new men and women. A recent example of simplicity would be Mother Teresa, whom Barron praises, saying, "No one in the last one hundred years propagated the Christian faith more effectively than this simple nun who lived in utter poverty."[22] These are extreme examples of living simplicity, and they remind us that the detachment from earthly riches is intimately connected with care and concern for the involuntarily poor. Bishop Barron commends the US bishops when they indicate that "every seminarian should have 'sustained contact with those who are privileged in God's eyes,' which is to say, 'the poor, the marginalized, the sick, and the suffering.'"[23]

The power of simplicity of life for the priest is to witness to the jaded world that "when we place God and God's purposes at the center of our lives, we can live happily with either wealth or poverty, with either fame or obscurity, with either power or weakness."[24] And the same is true for celibacy, the ability to live without sexual love and the comforts of family life. Yet neither celibacy nor simplicity will yield any kind of true Christian heroism without the joy and peace that can only come from a fruitful prayer life. Otherwise, they would be testaments only to our own stamina, not to the power and wisdom of God.

21. Robert Barron, *Renewing Our Hope: Essays for the New Evangelization* (Washington, DC: The Catholic University of America Press, 2020), 265.

22. Robert Barron with John L. Allen Jr., *To Light a Fire on the Earth: Proclaiming the Gospel in a Secular Age* (New York: Image Books, 2017), 69.

23. Barron, *Renewing Our Hope,* 185, quoting the *Program of Priestly Formation* 239, p. 81.

24. Robert Barron, *The Great Story of Israel: Election, Freedom, Holiness* (Park Ridge, IL: Word on Fire, 2022), 211. Bishop Barron observes this in light of the story of King Solomon.

ONE OF THE MAIN "JOBS" OF A PRIEST—TO PRAY!

For the priesthood to be attractive, we have to see God himself as attractive. In "The Priest as the Bearer of Mystery," Bishop Barron wonderfully draws out this mysterious otherness of God: "At the heart of the Christian faith is confrontation with the all-grounding and all-encompassing mystery of Being itself which is God. The believer is grasped, shaken, overwhelmed by that powerful force which, in Jesus Christ is revealed as passionate, unconditional love."[25]

Bishop Barron here recalls the ancient language of the Church Fathers, speaking of God in terms of "mystery," and of the priest as a "bearer" of this mystery. This does not mean, of course, that God is mystery in the sense of a puzzle to be solved, but it helps to remind us that—however long we have followed him and invoked his name—he is so much greater than we can understand or control! Bishop Barron says that the priest must therefore be an "authentically *religious* leader."[26] He must be a man conformed to Christ by prayer, an active mystic even in the midst of a busy ministry.

Here I must underline a point implicit in Bishop Barron's theology of the priesthood. The only way for a priest of Jesus Christ to be authentically religious is to pray. One of our main tasks as a priest is to pray! Prayer is not optional for any priest, be he a member of a religious order or a diocesan priest. The importance of prayer is brought out by the scholastic axiom *Nemo dat quod non habet,* which means "You can't give what you don't have." If we as priests don't rely on the mystery of God as something that is as necessary for our lives through prayer, how can we pass that reliance on to

25. Barron, *Bridging the Great Divide*, 228.

26. Barron, 230.

others in our ministries? If we as priests are not striving to receive grace in our own lives, then how can we expect our people to want to strive for holiness?

I hope it will seem to many readers that this point should hardly need emphasizing, but I assure you that it does. I remember concelebrating the Chrism Mass in my diocese a number of years ago, and our bishop asked us priests in his homily to spend at least fifteen minutes a day in private prayer before the Eucharist. I have to admit that I was surprised that this wasn't already happening in the lives of most priests. Fifteen minutes a day in quiet prayer, to me at least, really doesn't seem like all that much! When I was in high school, I had an amazing priest for junior year religion class. This young priest became a friend, a mentor, and a role model for me. In fact, he "vested me" (helped me into my vestments for the first time) at my priestly ordination—one of the biggest honors that could be given by a priest-to-be to an older priest. I recall speaking to this priest once about prayer in general and the prayer life of priests in particular when I was in the college-level seminary. Then he spoke some words that have remained with me over my twenty-five years as a priest: "If you're too busy to pray, then you're too busy! You have to drop something else out of the schedule that you're doing that's probably not essential." When I find I am too busy to pray, too busy to take even fifteen minutes for some quiet reflection, I ask myself, "What fills my time instead of prayer?" Usually, it is frivolous and frenetic activity that serves no ultimately good purpose. Even if it is something objectively good and wholesome, too bad. Without prayer, there's no strength to do a heroic amount of ministry.

When I meet with the seminarians who are assigned to me for formation, I try to encourage them to be men of prayer. With them,

I use the analogy of a chair to describe a good, healthy prayer life for a priest. A steady chair has a center, a seat, and four legs to support it. The seat, the center of the prayer life of the priest, is of course the daily celebration of the Mass. The Mass is the ultimate food for the journey of life. And even if there is no congregation, the priest can still offer Holy Mass, preferably with a server.

What are the legs that hold up the chair? One leg is the Liturgy of the Hours, that daily prayer that sanctifies our day, prayed on behalf of the whole world. In speaking as a seminarian with the young priest from my high school (who has since passed away), I told him that I was having a hard time praying the Liturgy of the Hours when I was not in community. He told me something that I will never forget: "The Liturgy of the Hours is essential for our prayer. We don't just pray it to sanctify our own day. It's in a way the bare minimum of our prayer life. It is what is required of us by our ordinations, and it is a joy to pray on behalf of the Church." The second leg is the Holy Rosary (or another Marian devotion), a way of imploring the gracious intercession of the Mother of God. The third leg is Eucharistic Adoration, spending some time in the true and Real Presence of the Lord, even if it is for only fifteen minutes a day. The final leg is spiritual reading, reflecting on Sacred Scripture, the writings of the Fathers of the Church and the saints, and other good material that can help us grow in the spiritual life. Remember Bishop Barron's insistence (and mine) that the life of the mind is essential to a fruitful spiritual life. Focusing only on good feelings and interior inspirations without nurturing sound theology will only lead one astray.

These spiritual pillars will not only feed the priest's own devotion but also dispose him to receive the gifts of the Holy Spirit that will show him how to lead other souls. The priest is one who not only bears the Mystery but leads others into the Mystery. This is the first of Bishop Barron's distinctive descriptions of the priest's task: mystagogue.

THE PRIEST AS MYSTAGOGUE

One of the problems with the notion of a "superhero" is that he or she is a person who not only stands apart from or above other people, but in a sense does all of the work for them. It is up to Iron Man or Superman to save the world from impossible forces, whereas regular folks have to sit around and hope they succeed. For a long time, this was a problem for many Catholics as regards the priesthood—the priest was the *alter Christus*, the other Christ, who would do all of the otherwise impossible religious tasks, while the layperson was doing well enough just to show up on Sundays, pay tithes, try to be good, and confess his or her sins when inevitably falling short. The notion was foreign that every Catholic should personally know God for himself or herself—even though it was taught in the *Baltimore Catechism* and repeated by Vatican II's "universal call to holiness."

For Bishop Barron, on the contrary, the goal of the priest is not to live in contact with the Mystery in place of his people, but to bring them too into living contact with the Mystery; in other words, "the priest of Jesus Christ is, first and foremost, a mystagogue." Mystagogy is an ancient term for the instruction that newly baptized Christians received after their initiation into the Church. "Before this, following the so-called 'discipline of the secret' (*Disciplina arcani*), they were kept hidden from them or only alluded to."[27]

27. Cardinal Raniero Cantalamessa, *The Power of the Cross: Good Friday Sermons from the Papal Preacher* (Park Ridge, IL: Word on Fire, 2022), 13.

Once they were admitted to "the sacred mysteries" of the Eucharistic liturgy, initiates—not only clergy—were considered partakers of the Mystery of God.

This term "mystagogy" has been revived today for the "post-baptismal catechesis" that takes place from Easter to Pentecost for those who join the Church as adults.[28] But Bishop Barron likes to use the term "mystagogue" in a more general sense because of its meaning in Greek as someone who "initiates others into" a mystery or mysteries.[29] In calling the priest a mystagogue "first and foremost," I think Bishop Barron is emphasizing that today, even though many Christians bring their bodies to church and perhaps even their hearts to the service of others, they have not opened their minds to "the ever-greater, always more alluring power of God,"[30] such that they are hardly better off than someone who has had no instruction in the sacraments![31]

As I discussed in chapter 1, Christianity is above all a way of seeing. Thus, the task of the priest as mystagogue, Bishop Barron explains, is "to hold up to the people of God the great images, stories, and pictures of salvation that are at the heart of the Christian tradition."[32] He is the man who is "entrusted with the sacred symbols

28. *United States Catholic Catechism for Adults* (Washington, DC: United States Conference of Catholic Bishops, 2006), 191.

29. Barron, *Bridging the Great Divide*, 228.

30. "How to Build a Better Priest," 11.

31. Considering a Pew Research poll of 2019 that indicated that nearly seven out of ten Catholics deny the Real Presence of Christ in the Eucharist (Gregory A. Smith, "Just One-Third of U.S. Catholics Agree with Their Church That Eucharist Is Body, Blood of Christ," Pew Research Center, August 5, 2019, https://www.pewresearch.org/fact-tank/2019/08/05/transubstantiation-eucharist-u-s-catholics/), this hardly seems an exaggeration. Indeed, because so many people today in places like Europe and North America have many years of education, they think they know more than they really do, which is even worse.

32. Barron, *Bridging the Great Divide*, 228–229.

and given the responsibility of making them speak."[33] According to Barron, the priest-mystagogue is called to become an exceptional preacher, one who cannot help but tell the Good News. Having been "conformed personally and existentially to that word, the priest speaks of and from the experience of being grasped by God."[34] The priest-mystagogue as a preacher is one who is "conformed to the Word that is Jesus Christ and must therefore be a lifelong student, not only of the Scripture, but of the great literary expressions of the Catholic sensibility."[35] Bishop Barron elaborates on this need to use all available intellectual and cultural tools in sharing the mystery of Christ with his people: "Catholic preachers do not subscribe to the Reformation principle of *sola scriptura* (Scripture alone); rather, they happily take advantage of the art, music, painting, poetry, philosophy, lives of the saints, and spirituality that serve as amplifications of the biblical message."[36] While no amount of knowing things will replace knowing Jesus, it is no accident that so many of the great preachers of the past, including "Origen, Augustine, Bernard, Thomas Aquinas . . . and John Henry Newman," had not only a deep spirituality but also a wide-ranging grasp of theology, philosophy, and more mundane pursuits like grammar, rhetoric, and even the natural sciences. In many ways, we can see that Barron's *CATHOLICISM* (2011), the documentary series that introduced him to the wider public, is his attempt precisely to model this mystagogy for the Church and the world.

The priest, configured to Jesus by his sacred ordination, teaches the faithful, like the Lord did, to open their eyes to the effects

33. Barron, 229.

34. Barron, 230.

35. Barron, 230.

36. Robert Barron, *Proclaiming the Power of Christ* (Park Ridge, IL: Word on Fire Institute, [2008] 2021), xv.

of the Spirit, to perceive the kingdom of God in their midst. I discussed in chapter 1 that this kingdom is Jesus Christ himself, in his Incarnation, which is the foundation for all of the sacraments. But that does not mean that we try to point to Jesus only in the sacraments themselves. Bishop Barron observes that some Catholics who have fallen in love with Jesus have come to "the point of admiration and worship, lost in wonder at the strange work that God has accomplished uniquely in Jesus of Nazareth."[37] If I were a parish priest, and this was a description of my parishioners, I would probably be turning somersaults! (Figuratively speaking.) But Bishop Barron is in fact describing what he considers an incomplete faith. Pushing us further, he notes that "Jesus nowhere in his Gospels urges his followers to worship him," but "he insistently calls them to *follow* him."[38] Barron explains that in Jesus' teaching, this kingdom, "the Incarnation, *is not something to be admired from the outside, but rather an energy in which to participate.*"[39] Hence, "in John's Gospel, Jesus speaks of himself as the vine *onto which we are grafted like branches*, and he compares himself to food *that we are to take into ourselves*. These beautifully organic images are meant to highlight our participation in the event of the Incarnation, our concrete citizenship in the kingdom of God."[40]

Unfortunately, most Catholics—even if in a state of grace—do not show awareness or fruits of living with this divine energy. Why is this?

In Barron's masterpiece *And Now I See*, he uses the image of the blind man Bartimaeus (Mark 10:46–52) as an image for the

37. Barron, *And Now I See*, xiii.

38. Barron, xiii–xiv.

39. Barron, xiii.

40. Barron, xiv.

overcoming of the paralysis of the heart brought on by sin and sadness.[41] Bartimaeus will follow Jesus on the way, but only after his eyes are *healed* can he *see* where he is going.[42] Hence, in order to fulfill his ministry as mystagogue, it is also the priest's role to be like Christ, the "healer of broken hearts and minds."[43] Bishop Barron calls such a priest "a doctor of the soul."

BECOMING A DOCTOR OF THE SOUL

When the Pharisees complained that Jesus was eating with tax collectors and sinners, he responded, "Those who are well have no need of a physician, but those who are sick; I have come to call not the righteous but sinners" (Mark 2:17). When Bishop Barron speaks of the priesthood as "soul doctoring," he has two aims in mind. First of all, he wants to highlight the connection between holiness and wholeness that Jesus references in this classic Gospel passage and which I discussed in chapter 2. Bishop Barron does not simply assume that today's people are spiritually sick because the Church says that we are sinners, or because we empirically see falling rates of Church membership and attendance as well as the rise of activity. He instead points, as an example, to the classic problem of concupiscence, which he describes as "an elemental spiritual desire" in which the "soul's infinite desire for God can get hooked onto something else: money, sex, power, possessions."[44] The destructive power of these false idols is evident in many ways in

41. A similar theme marks Bishop Barron's first book, *Thomas Aquinas: Spiritual Master* (Park Ridge, IL: Word on Fire Academic, [1996] 2021).

42. Barron, *And Now I See*, xviii–xix.

43. Barron, *Bridging the Great Divide*, 236.

44. "How to Build a Better Priest," 11.

contemporary culture. In *And Now I See*, against those who would see such problems as basically manageable by better government or psychology, he recounts the greatest evils of the twentieth century, from the Holocaust to the Rwandan genocide, and observes: "There seems to be something profoundly and dangerously *wrong* with us, a flaw that cannot be wished or thought away, an ineradicable darkness of the heart, a sickness of soul."[45] This is ultimately "a virus of the soul that will kill us spiritually and that we are incapable of eradicating ourselves."[46]

The second reason that Bishop Barron proposes "doctor of the soul" as a fitting title for the priest—and the dominant motivation he gives in his interview "How to Build a Better Priest"—is to emphasize the excitement of being on the front lines of this struggle to bring healing to people. Barron says, "I want to make the priesthood as exciting as being a brain surgeon, and as difficult and inspiring." Responding to the concern, "Doesn't it take an exceptionally wise and intelligent person to do this?" Bishop Barron doubles down: "Absolutely. . . . What's the difference between a doctor and a priest? As someone once answered long ago, there really is no comparison: one deals with matters of life and death; the other just deals with the health of the body."[47] The bishop's goal with this proposal was to be able to attract and inspire "the greatest minds" of the current generation to choose becoming a soul doctor over a medical doctor or some other intellectually demanding profession (law, finance, etc.), wagering that by making the priesthood more difficult and

45. Barron, *And Now I See*, 3.

46. Barron, 219.

47. "How to Build a Better Priest," 13.

even "elite," we would attract better—and more—candidates for vocations than by accepting mediocrity.

As a seminarian at the time, I was certainly inspired by this vision. Barron in particular inspired me to reconsider the importance of the theology I was learning. I began to see it, perhaps for the first time, as a powerful tool in extending Jesus' *healing* ministry. All those hours of study and reading now seemed worth it for the life of the priest in light of the words of this young theologian, for it is he who is Truth who is also the "healer of broken hearts and minds."[48]

But the reader may also recall from chapter 1 that I said that the priesthood need not be reserved to geniuses but merely those open to developing their intellectual life of faith. I do believe my position can be harmonized with Bishop Barron's notion of how we should present the priesthood attractively in the sense of becoming a "soul doctor." We do want the young minds capable of being brain surgeons to see that there is a path of profound intellectual engagement in the Church that will nevertheless help people as much or more than going to medical school. We can engage the Church's best and brightest especially when we teach them to imitate the great theologians of the Church's tradition, Barron writes, because "they were not writing to get their articles published in learned journals. The Fathers of the Church and the medieval theologians wrote as pastors and ministers; they worried about the care of souls. That is precisely what the priest does[:] doctor that deepest part of the person we call the soul. That's something that makes priesthood fascinating and indispensable, without being exclusive or clerical."[49]

48. Barron, *Bridging the Great Divide*, 236.

49. "How to Build a Better Priest," 11.

But, on the other hand, just as not every doctor performs brain surgery or writes in medical journals, not every priest needs a doctorate in theology or needs to write in academic journals. Plenty of priests are needed to be "general practitioners" in parish ministry or religious life. This does not mean there is not an "elite" component; for ordination, we certainly require a number of years of schooling, which means there is a floor of natural intelligence and studiousness necessary to enter the priesthood. However, the truly attractive part of becoming priests of Jesus Christ is that he clothes us with *his* wisdom and *his* intelligence, making up for whatever we lack—provided, of course, that we remain within him through prayer.

Those qualifications aside, what does it mean to act as a soul doctor? Barron defines the soul as "that still-point at the heart of every person, that deepest center, that point of encounter with the transcendent yet incarnate mystery of God."[50] Or to put in another way, "the ground and source of all psychological and physical energy; it is the matrix and organizing power of the human person."[51] In order to reach this deep center of the person, "the theologian or pastor studies theological anthropology in order to learn what makes souls sick or healthy."[52] He can look at the symptoms the person is presenting—loneliness, confusion, anger, sadness, disappointment—but he must go deeper, finding the causes of these maladies. Some of this work is painful, as it must "bring us face-to-face with the inner darkness," "convince us of our helplessness," and "consequently

50. Barron, *Bridging the Great Divide*, 236.

51. Barron, 236.

52. Barron, *And Now I See*, xxvi.

open us up to grace."[53] This "looking at sin has a transformative and ultimately salvific purpose," but it requires overcoming "the conviction that one can save oneself through heroic moral effort or mystical insight or flights of theoretical knowledge."[54] Some of this work is encouraging, as it involves "raising to the surface the godlike quality in us," to "stir up that longing for God that remains despite the dysfunction" in order to "prepare the way for transformation of the soul."[55]

"Soul doctoring" happens in the priest's pastoral work among the people of God. In the first place, it occurs in catechesis and preaching. It certainly occurs when the priest celebrates the sacraments. The diagnosis of the individual soul takes place in "pastoral work, in hospital visits, in preparing people for the sacraments, in counseling." What medicines are in the pharmacy of the "soul doctor"? Nothing less than "the great doctrines, teachings, spiritual writings, and images of our tradition" that are held up by the priest as mystagogue. In *And Now I See*, Barron specifically brings out the healing power of the doctrines of the simplicity of God, the commandment against idolatry, the omnipresence and omnipotence of God, the kingliness of God, the lowliness of God, the naming of God, the Trinity, and even the problem of evil.[56] In each of these cases, he engages with these doctrines not in some flat recitation from a *Catechism* but with a rich reflection on a classic text either from Scripture or a great theologian. And the salves are not limited to doctrines; in that book, he also cites medieval rose windows

53. Barron, 7–8.

54. Barron, 38.

55. Barron, 44–45.

56. Barron, 104–150.

and the fiction of Flannery O'Connor.[57] In essence, according to Barron, "You use psychology and every other tool you can, but in the end what you hold up is the transforming power of Christ, the Incarnation."[58]

As such, the priest, on the one hand, needs to draw as widely as possible from the truths of faith and the history of Catholic culture in a way appropriate to the person or audience at hand; but on the other hand, he does not set up his own intelligence or generosity as a replacement for Christ; rather, he acts in the *person of Christ* as a kind of channel for divine grace. Barron writes, "We heal the soul by bringing to bear the *salvator,* the healer, the one who in his person reconciled God and us, who opened soul to the divine power."[59] The priest, through the sacraments, the sacred liturgy, the Christian tradition, the Christian imagination, and in and through the doctrine of the Church, becomes the one who is a "bearer of the new being." These medicines are "symbols of transformation" whose primary purpose is to change the lives of Christians by drawing them into the *imitatio Christi.*"[60]

CONCLUSION

This chapter has shown that, far from seeing pastoral ministry as divorced from the intellect, the two core concepts of Bishop Barron's unique theology of the priesthood—as mystagogue and soul doctor—are as inseparable from the priest's intellectual training as his spiritual training. As preacher and teacher, the priest must not

57. Barron, 170, 192.

58. "How to Build a Better Priest," 11.

59. Barron, *Bridging the Great Divide*, 236.

60. Barron, 237.

only prophetically speak the Word of God but also lead his people into a real contact with the unfathomable Mystery through "the great images, stories, and pictures of salvation that are at the heart of the Christian tradition." To call the priest a mystagogue is to recognize that we Christians—even well-educated priests—never really lose our status as beginners before the infinite Mystery of God, beggars for divine grace, wisdom, and understanding; we are always like those catechumens in the early Church whose eyes are being opened through contact with the sacraments and other instruments of divine grace.

And we are always in need of healing—of our spiritual eyes, ears, hands, legs, and every other part of us. It is for this reason that Barron calls the priest a "doctor of the soul," to recognize as Jesus did that the work of sanctifying is for us sinners a work of healing. Barron develops the idea of the doctor of the soul as prescribing the medicine of Christian doctrine, using the theological concepts of the Incarnation, divine simplicity, and the absolutely gratuitous nature of creation to heal the sin-sick soul. For Barron, these concepts and all the rich articles of the faith are indeed icons, ones that "illumine and open up the spirit."[61] They show each man and woman his or her own particular share in human misery but also in the greatness of human destiny. Bishop Barron observes that "soul-doctoring is needed because of the *pusilla anima*," but "it is possible because of the seeds of the *magna anima*" in every human being.[62]

As priests, we have to embody for our people the overcoming of the *pusilla anima* and the discovering of the *magna anima* through the animating power of Christ. We have to do so by lives of prayer,

61. Barron, 243.

62. Barron, *And Now I See*, 58.

celibacy, and simplicity, eschewing any excuses that because we made big sacrifices (career, family), we are empowered to live with a thousand small indulgences of gadgets, fine foods, fancy cars, or time-sucking entertainments. We must do so by exercising our Christ-given works of priesthood, prophecy, and kingship, leading our people but also listening to them and trying to foster their charisms rather than substituting for them. We have to do so by embracing the Church as one, holy, catholic, and apostolic, even in our time of extreme confusion and trial for the institutions of the Church (even those that are self-inflicted). We must do so by becoming mystagogues and soul doctors in ways appropriate to the ministries to which we are called. And we should do so by learning from Bishop Barron's words and from his example.

Saying yes to these roles will mean saying no to others. Bishop Barron acknowledged that "the pastoral demands are so enormous that I'm sure many priests think they have no time to spend with the tradition, with art and architecture and philosophy and drama." But he responded by saying that if the priest is clear about what he is uniquely able to provide, he will have to be willing and in fact eager to cede other roles to lay people and deacons, citing the creation of the diaconate in the Acts of the Apostles for a similar reason—to free up the Apostles to serve the word of God.[63] Doing so will mean avoiding unnecessarily becoming a hyphenated priest, as I discussed in chapter 1, which means to keep side ministries to a reasonable amount of time and energy. Bishop Barron himself, for instance, says that he spends only about 10 percent of his time on his ministry Word on Fire.

63. "How to Build a Better Priest," 13.

If we do these things, we will find that it is not only possible but likely that we can live a heroic priesthood that can bring grace to God's people and attract others to this vocation. Like Peter Parker from his spider bite or Captain America from his supersoldier serum, the priest is given powers—supernatural gifts—beyond our natural abilities, and the call to use them for the good of the community. Unlike most of those fictional heroes, however, and more like surgeons, soldiers, pilots, and others who are given positions of great responsibility in the real world, priests receive a great deal of training and formation in all dimensions of their lives—human, spiritual, intellectual, and pastoral—before they are asked to wield their gifts in active ministry. The remainder of this book will examine each of those areas of formation in light of the foundations of priestly identity established in this first part of the book.

PART II

Priestly Formation

INTRODUCTION TO PART II

The Four Dimensions of Priestly Formation

We have seen in the first three chapters of this book the essential outline of the priesthood. I hope there are at least some readers whose response is "Terrific! When can I start?" Zeal for Christ and for the service of the Church is a beautiful thing, but for young men discerning the priesthood, the answer is always, "Years from now." The Church does not merely hire or recruit men for the priesthood; it takes care in selecting them through a shared process of discernment, and an even greater care in *forming* them, in helping them shape each dimension of their lives in conformity to Christ. As we will see, the Church prudently focuses on four dimensions in the formation of the priest: the human, spiritual, intellectual, and pastoral dimensions. This is one of the reasons that studying for the priesthood takes so much time: in the United States, it is a minimum of eight years—and often more! Over the course of the next several chapters, we are going to look at these dimensions of priestly formation one by one.

WHY IT TAKES SO LONG TO BECOME A PRIEST

Given the great need for priests to minister to the faithful, the question might then be asked: Does it have to take that long? What are they teaching you for so many years? There is plenty of academic learning—a program of study specified by the US bishops' *Program of Priestly Formation* gives pride of place to philosophy (two years) and theology (four years). This period also involves learning the rituals of the Church: how to celebrate Mass, hear confessions, anoint, baptize, preach, and perform marriages. Nevertheless, more than just being an intellectual or practical education, the time of preparation for the priesthood is an integral formation. In fact, far from trying to speed things up, the Vatican's Congregation for the Clergy has recently asked for a mandatory "propaedeutic stage" of at least a year prior to the beginning of studies, and a "vocational synthesis stage" of at least a year in ministry after seminary studies and ordination to the diaconate. These are now incorporated into the sixth edition of the US bishops' *Program of Priestly Formation*. One introductory year, two years of philosophy, four years of theology, and a year in ministry is how we get to the "new normal" of eight years.

Even though the first and final years were not required when I was coming through as a seminarian, I spent even more time in seminary than that.[1] For young men who feel the call to the priesthood at an early age, a first stop after discussion with families and the diocesan director of vocations is often a college-level seminary or a house of formation connected to a university. In my case, when

1. For me personally, if you were to add up the time that I spent in the seminary before ordination, it would be eight years. Counting my unique high school experience, you would have to add another four, bringing it to twelve!

I graduated from high school, I went to St. John's University in New York City and lived at our diocesan house of formation. There, I lived in common with other young (and some not-so-young) men, all of whom were discerning a priestly vocation. Through regular spiritual direction and formation advising with some fine priests on the seminary staff, I learned more about the daily life of a priest and, perhaps even more importantly, I learned how to pray not only the Liturgy of the Hours (the Divine Office)—which is the duty of the ordained—but to speak in quiet with the Lord and rest in his presence. Years later, when I was teaching high school, I was invited to teach some theology classes part-time in the same college-level seminary program that I had attended many years before.

From there, I was assigned to the next stage of priestly formation: the major-level seminary. Although I had expected to be assigned to a local seminary in New York, I was asked to go to the Pontifical North American College in Rome (NAC). There, I had a number of life-changing experiences that broadened my worldview and truly confirmed my priestly vocation. When asked what I learned in the major seminary, I like to say that I learned to *be* a priest there. After four years at this seminary, during which time I received my theological education at the Pontifical Gregorian University, I was ordained a priest. Leaving the NAC (*knack*, as it is called), I never expected to be back, and yet, I was blessed to serve for several years on the formation faculty there as a formation advisor and as the seminary's academic dean. Most recently, I was called back to New York to teach at the archdiocesan seminary of Saint Joseph's in Dunwoodie, Yonkers. Counting my time in high school, in one way, shape, or form I have been in a seminary or a seminary-like environment since 1986, with the exception of five very happy and fulfilling years in a big, active parish in my diocese.

Those "seminary" years include the time when I was a young priest and my bishop assigned me to teach full-time in our diocesan high school and prep seminary program. The school was, by and large, a regular boys' Catholic high school where the students lived at their own homes with their parents and commuted daily. They had priests, religious, and lay women and men as teachers in class; attended daily Mass and weekly Adoration of the Blessed Sacrament; and met with a priest on the faculty a few times a year to discuss the possibility of a priestly vocation.

Believe me, there was no hard sell to these young men about the priesthood. All that was asked of them was an openness to thinking about the vocation. The vast majority of graduates of this school did not go on to the college-level seminary, and even among those who did go to the college-level, there were many who were not ordained priests. And that's perfectly fine! One cannot take a fourteen-year-old and make him into a priest. That idea is patently absurd. The purpose of any vocational recruitment program for young men is simply to expose them to belief in God in an age that so militates against it; to the beauty and wonder of the Church, especially in the daily miracle of Holy Mass; and to the fact that, by and large, priests are normal, happy, healthy men striving for holiness and service to God's people.[2]

In fact, I would say that—despite the challenges that I discussed in chapter 2—few people today are better prepared for a happy life

2. That today's Catholic priests generally live happy and fulfilled—if sometimes stressful—lives has been confirmed time and again, including by The Catholic University of America's "National Study of Catholic Priests" in 2022, https://catholicproject.catholic.edu/national-study-of-catholic-priests/.

than priests. Brain surgeons and elite pilots may be hyper-prepared to keep their patients or their passengers alive, but what other vocation spends so much time not only learning how to work but how to live and love? And probably only the modern military takes as much care with the psychological and social aspects of its workforce as the Catholic Church now does with its priests. As Bishop Barron observes, even to enter the seminary during his time as rector, "criminal background checks, careful psychological screening, and numerous interviews were *de rigueur* for every candidate."[3] Perhaps in the past there was a two-dimensional focus on only intellectual and spiritual matters—which may have contributed to the twentieth-century crisis among the clergy—but today, from Vatican directives down to each diocese's and local seminary's internal guidelines, there is an emphasis on holistic development along four dimensions of priestly formation: human, spiritual, intellectual, and pastoral. This is not to say things never go wrong—every seminarian and priest has free will after all—but the general quality of men being ordained today shows the value of this careful process.

Each of these dimensions builds upon the other. In human formation, the man who feels called by the Lord to examine a priestly vocation attempts to strengthen his own personal identity. He has to be a holistic, happy, healthy human being, a man properly ordered. If not, how can he give his life away in service to others? We have mentioned already the old scholastic axiom *Nemo dat quod non habet* (You can't give what you don't have). Unless the foundation is secure and strong, how can a house, a temple for the Lord, be built? This human formation asks the man, like the Delphic Oracle

3. Robert Barron, *Letter to a Suffering Church: A Bishop Speaks on the Sexual Abuse Crisis* (Park Ridge, IL: Word on Fire, 2019), 84.

did, to "know thyself." He is called not to ignore any issues that are troubling him but to deal with them in a constructive manner. This human formation includes growth in his physical, emotional, and psychological health as well as in his learning to live as a chaste celibate man. In his human formation, the seminarian moves from self-knowledge to self-acceptance to self-gift. He learns to practice the cardinal virtues of justice, prudence, temperance, and fortitude as well as the theological virtues of faith, hope, and charity.

In spiritual formation, the man who feels called by the Lord to examine a priestly vocation pursues growth in his relationship with Christ. Through prayer and through the guidance of a seminary-appointed spiritual director, he seeks to put on the mind of Christ Jesus and renounce self-centeredness. Through prayer, the frequenting of the sacraments, and the guidance of the seminary formators, the man allows himself to be known by Christ and awaits Christ with a listening heart.

In intellectual formation, the man who feels called by the Lord to examine a priestly vocation learns more and more about the One who knows him and who loves him better than anyone else in the world: the Lord Jesus. He learns all about theology, which comes from the Greek words *theos* and *logos*, meaning "God's word." By God's word, I mean so much more than Sacred Scripture; I mean God's Word made flesh, Jesus Christ our Lord. As I discussed in the introduction, knowing the Lord in his divine and human being has a strong intellectual dimension, and grasping these truths requires not only the sacred science of theology but the human "love of wisdom" studied through philosophy. And, having learned about theology and philosophy and other necessary subjects, he then learns to communicate that understanding to a world that so desperately needs it.

In pastoral formation, the man who feels called by the Lord to examine a priestly vocation finds that this is where the "rubber meets the road." Here, he has the opportunity to discern how best to be of service to God's people, putting into action what he has learned and who he has become through his human, spiritual, and intellectual formation. As he becomes a shepherd of God's flock, he seeks to live as "a man after God's own heart" (1 Sam. 13:14).

In this and the next three chapters, I will continue to make reference to the thought of Robert Barron, who for most of his priesthood has been involved in seminary formation. Thus, seminary formation was the context in which he developed the theology of the priesthood that I have been unpacking throughout this book. For many years, Barron served as a professor of systematic theology at the University of Saint Mary of the Lake / Mundelein Seminary outside of Chicago. In 2012, Cardinal Francis George appointed then-Fr. Barron to become the Rector-President of the seminary and university. To be a rector of a seminary requires a priest who is more than just a capable administrator. It requires a priest who is more than just a learned academic and a good teacher. It requires a priest who is able to establish "a profound and loyal cooperation" with those responsible for each of these four dimensions of formation because he is, in himself, a model of priesthood,[4] a priest who is capable of being the father of a community of men who are themselves studying to be "fathers." There is an old expression in

4. Congregation for the Clergy, *The Gift of the Priestly Vocation* (*Ratio Fundamentalis Institutionis Sacerdotalis*) 134, December 7, 2016, http://www.clerus.va/content/dam/clerus/Ratio%20Fundamentalis/The%20Gift%20of%20the%20Priestly%20Vocation.pdf.

seminary formation: "As goes the rector, so goes the seminary." By all accounts, Mundelein Seminary was in fine hands with Fr. Barron as the priest model and paterfamilias.

Ultimately, if you the reader are a man who attends or is considering joining a Catholic seminary, you will learn a great deal about all the aspects of formation from your own rector, formators, professors, and other influences. You should also read—repeatedly!— St. John Paul II's *Pastores Dabo Vobis* (1992),[5] the new sixth edition of the US Conference of Catholic Bishops' *Program of Priestly Formation* (2022), and the Congregation for the Clergy's *The Gift of the Priestly Vocation* (2016). These are the official, authoritative sources that I will discuss below. Nevertheless, official documents don't always make for page-turners. I hope in the following pages to give some inspiring and useful insights into this process from Robert Barron's theology and my own experience.

Two things to remember: The first is the old adage that the seminarian you are is the priest you will be. Please pray for seminarians. As one who is engaged as a formator in a major seminary, I can truly attest that we have heroic men in the seminary, men striving for sanctity of life and trying to be holistic men for Christ and his Church. And please don't just pray for "more" vocations. We don't just need more numbers, despite the tremendous need for priests in the world; what we need are happy, holy, healthy priests.

Second, as the rector and seminary formators act, so the seminarians will do, often in reaction. Please pray for me and other seminary formators. We have to be the best priests we can be because we need to help the Lord form priests for the future, and, in

5. John Paul II, *Pastores Dabo Vobis*, apostolic exhortation, March 25, 1992, vatican.va.

doing so, help to assure that our Mother, the Church, can offer her children shepherds after the Sacred Heart of Christ. Fr. Jean-Jacques Olier (the founder of the Society of St. Sulpice, a group of priests dedicated to the formation of future priests) had one main desire for his seminary formators: that they would want "to live supremely for God in Christ Jesus our Lord, so much so that the inner life of His only Son should penetrate to the inmost depths of our heart and to such an extent that everyone should be able to say, 'It is no longer I who live, but Christ who lives in me' (Gal. 2:20)." It is a heavy responsibility and even a burden, but it is also a true joy, and I, for one, am grateful to take part in the modern seminary system.

And I am grateful to St. Charles Borromeo for his foundation of this system several centuries ago. In discussing human formation, I want to begin by discussing why the seminary was created in hopes of continuing its mission today.

CHAPTER 4

The Human Dimension

We think that the formation of priests is hard today. The sixth edition of the *Program of Priestly Formation* explains the need for that initial "propaedeutic" year at the beginning of seminary formation by commenting, "A significant imbalance is present between the lifestyle promoted by contemporary society and priestly formation."[1] You can say that again! The seminarians I work with have had access to temptations in a way that I couldn't have imagined in my younger years, even just a couple of decades ago. Some people talk about the propaedeutic year as the year to detox from social media and turn off one's iPhone and pray. There's a lot of truth to that.

But a bit of historical perspective shows that the formation of future priests has always been difficult. In the sixteenth century, St. Charles Borromeo (1538–1584) recognized what was happening to the priests of his day. Some were lax, lazy, and lethargic, unable to articulate the great mysteries that had been handed on to them. Some were basically functionaries, celebrating Mass after Mass, and

1. *Program of Priestly Formation* 119, 6th ed. (Washington, DC: United States Conference of Catholic Bishops, 2022).

taking stipend after stipend, by and large concerned with the things of this world rather than the things of the world to come. Many were "secular" priests—that is, diocesan priests like myself, living in the *saecula* (the world)—but some were becoming truly secular in the worst sense of the word. And even some of the priests in religious orders—including the mendicant friars––weren't much better. These bad examples were certainly of no help as the Church was dealing with the upheaval of the Protestant Reformation.

The priesthood was in a sad state, and it had everything to do with how men were chosen and prepared for the priesthood. A family would go and apprentice a boy to a parish priest for a few years and, having paid the priest a hefty dowry, leave him there to learn. Often, these priests would let their young charges go throughout Europe, sowing their wild oats, and, without any level of formation, they would return to the priest, who would then go and recommend to the local bishop that he should ordain these young men.

Responding to the call of the Council of Trent (1545–1563) for a better priestly formation, St. Charles saw the need for a dedicated space, a seminary (meaning "seed-bed"), where young men could come together for true formation. This would not simply be a functional formation of how to do the things that priests do, but more importantly an instruction in who they were becoming. The seminary would teach them about their priestly ontology, and to always value being over doing.

St. Charles' basic model of seminary is what we have today around the world. I am blessed to have attended the seminaries that I did, all enriching me at the level of formation I needed, and I have been doubly blessed to have served as a faculty member of some of the seminaries that formed me. The good news is that we, too, live in a period of renewal in priestly formation, which also began with an ecumenical council—in this case, the Second Vatican Council. *Optatam Totius*, Vatican II's Decree on Priestly Training, was promulgated by Pope St. Paul VI on October 28, 1966.[2] Soon after the conclusion of the council, the US Bishops released the first edition of *The Program of Priestly Formation*. In 2022, the United States Conference of Catholic Bishops released its sixth edition of this guiding document, which was revised in keeping with "The Gift of the Priestly Vocation," the 2016 version of the *Ratio Fundamentalis Institutionis Sacerdotalis* released by the Vatican's Congregation for the Clergy.[3]

To my mind, though, the biggest "game-changer" in priestly formation occurred when Pope St. John Paul II released his post-synodal apostolic exhortation *Pastores Dabo Vobis* ("I Will Give You Shepherds") on March 25, 1992. This magnificent document outlines the Church's expectation for the integral formation of Catholic priests, and it is indeed a gift to the universal Church from John Paul II. *Pastores Dabo Vobis* transformed the notion of seminary formation in the minds of many from being merely a time of following the rules and learning the manuals to a truly holistic

2. *Optatam Totius*, in *The Word on Fire Vatican II Collection: Decrees and Declarations*, ed. Matthew Levering (Park Ridge, IL: Word on Fire Institute, 2023), 239–272. For more on this document, see Robert Barron, "*Optatam Totius* and the Renewal of the Priesthood," in *Renewing Our Hope: Essays for the New Evangelization* (Washington, DC: The Catholic University of America, 2020), 169–192.

3. It also reflects Benedict XVI's apostolic letter *Ministororum Institutio* (January 16, 2013). According to the prefect of the Congregation for the Clergy, Cardinal Beniamino Stella, the newest *Ratio* follows closely Pope Francis' own lived experience of priesthood by articulating Francis' concerns regarding the need for priests to avoid "temptations tied to money, to the authoritarian exercise of power, to rigid legalism and to vainglory" ("Vatican Issues New Guidelines for Priestly Formation," *Zenit*, December 9, 2016, https://zenit.org/articles/vatican-issues-new-guidelines-for-priestly-formation/).

period of formation, consisting of the four pillars (human, spiritual, intellectual, and pastoral) that I have already mentioned.

WHAT WE MEAN BY HUMAN FORMATION

The seminary requires a holistic development of the whole man in terms of his growth in the areas of human, spiritual, intellectual, and pastoral formation. It's a long journey! Formation is the process of disintegrating the individual as formed by worldly influences and reintegrating the individual according to the model of Jesus Christ. It is the process of "breaking the pot" and reshaping it according to the Church's template. And these pots that present themselves to us for ordination today were hardened so much earlier than even my generation twenty-five years ago; in an age of confused masculinity, with no father figures for many of them; with notions of sexuality warped by pornography; with childhoods of either privilege or deprivation, of either helicoptering or absent or even abusive parents. We who serve as seminary formators have our work cut out for us! These are the "human" issues that present themselves in seminary formation. It is up to seminary formators to try—despite our own weaknesses—to offer, in our own lives and examples, a priestly role model whom the seminarian can truly call "Father."

In *Pastores Dabo Vobis*, John Paul II placed human formation first, explaining that "the whole work of priestly formation would be deprived of its necessary foundation if it lacked a suitable human formation."[4] While the priesthood is fundamentally the grace of a sacrament, to quote another great scholastic adage, "Grace builds

4. John Paul II, *Pastores Dabo Vobis* 43, apostolic exhortation, March 25, 1992, vatican.va. This quote is itself one of the propositions put forward at the synod of bishops that preceded the document.

on nature." The *Program of Priestly Formation* observes, "As the humanity of the Word made flesh was the *instrumentum salutis*, so the humanity of the priest is instrumental in mediating the redemptive gifts of Christ to people today."[5] The human formation of a priest cannot be separated from his spiritual and intellectual life, nor from his pastoral ministry, but it can be distinguished from them to look at particular virtues and problems. The *PPF* lists ten human qualities seminaries should seek to foster in their priests: a conscience with openness to conversion; prudence and discernment; capacity for communion; effective communication; affective (emotional) maturity; respect for one's body (including physical health); capacity to relate well to others (including those from diverse backgrounds); stewardship of material possessions; fitness for a public role in the life of the Church; and chastity.[6]

The task of developing these human qualities is given its own section in documents about priestly formation, distinct from sections about spiritual, intellectual, or pastoral formation; but even more importantly, it is baked into the formation process by means of certain institutional arrangements. Among the priests involved in seminary formation, there is an important distinction between those who serve in the "external forum" and those who serve in the "internal forum." The external forum is basically the observable aspects of a seminarian's formation—primarily his growth in his human formation as well as his academic performance and his personal conduct. The priest who serves in this capacity in the seminary is called a formation advisor. He writes a report about

5. *Program of Priestly Formation* 182.

6. *Program of Priestly Formation* 183, 186.

the seminarian for the rector and for the seminary's bishop, and he votes on the advancement of the seminarian to the next year of formation. His vote as a formation advisor in most seminaries is advisory to the rector, whose decision, in turn, is advisory to the seminarian's bishop. Because of his supervisory relationship with the seminarian, the formation advisor cannot hear the confessions of seminarians under his authority.

The internal forum, in its essence, involves growth in the interior life of the seminarian. The priest who serves in this capacity is called a spiritual director. In many cases, the spiritual director also serves as the confessor to the seminarian. The spiritual director does not vote on the seminarian's advancement to Holy Orders and is required to keep all that is revealed to him in spiritual direction with strict confidence. The distinction of the two forums—internal and external—gives the seminarian a "safe space" in which to share his innermost feelings and movements of the Spirit (the internal forum), while also allowing the seminary a way (the external forum) to keep a close watch on his development and ensure that he is moving along the right track. This distinction between the two forums is rooted in canon law, and it also serves to protect the seminarian from spiritual and psychological abuse: he does not have to share his innermost thoughts with those who control his future, while he has an external authority to which he can appeal if he is uncomfortable with the personal advice of his spiritual director.

In my experience, it is nevertheless important in healthy settings that the seminarian is not bifurcated, revealing one face to his formation advisor and another to his spiritual director. These two forums, internal and external, are basically two sides of the same coin. The seminarian speaks of similar things, but in different manners, with his spiritual director and his formation advisor. The greater intimacy of the internal forum is not for the purpose of hiding and covering up problematic behavior; transparency is key. If the seminarian is to become a priest who is a "soul doctor," as Bishop Barron suggests, he must first be willing to bring forward his own wounds for healing. It is true that there is a risk that, by showing his human failings and struggles, the seminarian might even endanger the possibility of his ordination to the priesthood. But I have to say, that's okay! It's far better for both the Church and the man himself to determine at the time of seminary that certain necessary human elements are missing from his life, rather than to get ordained and have those failings drag down not only his own priesthood but the people of God entrusted to his care. The more likely scenario, though, is that when he seeks help, the good formators at the seminary will guide him toward entering the priesthood in a healthier state, emotionally and psychologically as well as spiritually and intellectually.

The US bishops' *Program of Priestly Formation* introduces its chapter on human formation by stating, "The foundation and center of all human formation is the Word made flesh."[7] In *Gaudium et Spes* 22, a passage Bishop Barron calls "a leitmotif and hermeneutical key for John Paul II,"[8] the fathers of the Second Vatican Council affirmed that "only in the mystery of the incarnate Word does the mystery of man take on light." What does Christ teach us about our humanity? *Gaudium et Spes* 24 continues, "Man . . . cannot fully find himself except through a sincere gift of himself." Pope St. John Paul II describes the necessity that a man who would present himself and be presented as a candidate for Holy Orders be a fully actualized human

7. *Program of Priestly Formation* 181.

8. Robert Barron, *Bridging the Great Divide: Confessions of a Post-Liberal, Post-Conservative Evangelical Catholic* (Lanham, MD: Rowman & Littlefield, 2004), 15.

being, a man who is secure in his affective maturity. He writes: "The Letter to the Hebrews clearly affirms the 'human character' of God's minister: he comes from the human community and is at its service, imitating Jesus Christ 'who in every respect has been tempted as we are, yet without sin' (Heb. 4:15)."[9]

Jesus Christ, he who is fully divine and fully human, is the model of all human beings. Human formation in seminary is a process of learning to imitate his humanity in all aspects of our life. The *Program of Priestly Formation* describes a process of "self-awareness" leading to "self-acceptance," "self-possession," and ultimately "self-gift."[10] Each of these stages has a certain resonance with a key theological motif in Bishop Barron's thinking. Self-awareness, more than just introspection, comes from the encounter with the kingdom of God in Jesus; second, to find true self-acceptance, we need to regain our center, recalling that we are made in the image and likeness of God; third, to gain true self-possession, we rely not on our own strength but on the dynamic of the Incarnation as "*not something to be admired from the outside, but rather an energy in which to participate*";[11] and fourth and finally, in order to enact a true self-gift as priests, we need to overcome fear and move from the *pusilla anima* to the *magna anima*.

SELF-AWARENESS

Growth in self-awareness should occur throughout the Christian life in general and throughout seminary formation and priestly life in particular. Nevertheless, I think it's fair to say that the first

9. John Paul II, *Pastores Dabo Vobis* 5.

10. *Program of Priestly Formation* 193.

11. Barron, *And Now I See: A Theology of Transformation* (Park Ridge, IL: Word on Fire Academic, [1998] 2021), 3.

(now mandatory) stage of seminary formation—the propaedeutic stage—is especially important as a time of self-discovery, free from the requirements of a full course load or other chores that might distract the prospective priest from what is really occurring in his heart and in his soul. The *Program of Priestly Formation* observes that "during this time, it should become clear whether he has the qualities and the maturity to integrate the four dimensions of priestly formation going forward."[12]

Part of building this self-awareness is uncovering what Deacon Edward J. McCormack calls "the vast, hidden, and complex world" that each seminarian "carries within him."[13] This includes his "hidden past"—the animal instincts of fallen human nature, the formative events of his childhood (some forgotten), and the "long-learned values, assumptions, and prejudices" of his cultural background; the "hidden present" with the operations of the unconscious mind, implicit learning, and ingrained habits (especially regarding technology); and "the hidden future," the underlying goals and motivations that shape his reactions, hopes and fears, and imaginations.[14] Deacon McCormack suggests that "a large part of formation involves identifying the values and assumptions a man has learned from our culture and where they stand in the face of the values of the kingdom of God."[15]

Here, I would like to recall Bishop Barron's argument that the kingdom of God is best understood as "the person of Jesus himself."[16]

12. *Program of Priestly Formation* 122.

13. Edward McCormack, *A Guide to Formation Advising for Seminary Faculty: Accompaniment, Participation, and Evaluation* (Washington, DC: The Catholic University of America Press, 2020), 109.

14. McCormack, 110–117.

15. McCormack, 114.

16. Barron, *And Now I See*, xiii.

The challenge of building self-awareness for a seminarian, therefore, is that of letting the light of Jesus illuminate the nooks and crannies of his past, present, and future, and of turning away from whatever in his life would block the conformity of his person to the ministry of Jesus Christ. As useful as psychology, sociology, and other human sciences can be, what is required for seminary formation is a fully integrated theological anthropology, humanity seen in the light of God. Barron defines it this way:

> Theological *anthropology* teaches us who we are in the presence of the divine—that is to say, at the level of *soul*. It analyzes the soul and learns its movements, its longings, its hopes, its typical problems, and its anxieties. Just as the medical doctor studies biology in order to learn how the body functions, so the theologian or pastor studies theological anthropology in order to learn what makes souls sick or healthy. In the terms of our discussion, the theological anthropologist examines the dynamics of *metanoia* and awakening to faith.[17]

Even though most seminarians have entered the seminary with a generous heart and an eagerness to follow Jesus, that zeal does not mean their souls are in fact healthy. I'll repeat the understatement I cited above from the *Program of Priestly Formation*: "A significant imbalance is present between the lifestyle promoted by contemporary society and priestly formation."[18] Conversion to Christ—*metanoia*—is not simply a change in behavior from a certain list of easily identifiable external sins; it is, as Barron puts it, a "change of vision

17. Barron, xxvi.

18. *Program of Priestly Formation* 119.

and consciousness."[19] It then has to sink in, as Deacon McCormack observes, at the level of "the heart, the imagination, and the hidden unconscious world"[20]—that is, the soil of the heart to which Jesus refers in his parable of the sower and the seed (Matt. 13:1–9, 18–23).

Even an outwardly pious seminarian can come to realize that his "ultimate concern" is not God but some lesser value. Thomas Aquinas, in his famous "Treatise on Happiness," identifies multiple pretenders for the ultimate end of the human person: wealth, honor, fame (or glory), power, pleasure, health, or some other good of the soul, such as knowledge or self-righteousness.[21] Any of these less-than-God motives could even be the driving reason that a man has entered the seminary. Perhaps the man is really seeking people's applause or the job security of a stable organization. These motivations are less likely in our time than in Charles Borromeo's time perhaps, but there can be subtler temptations. For instance, in a culture that values pleasure above all else, a young man experiencing conversion may reject worldly values, but only by switching from hedonism to the opposite error of rigorism. The moral rigorist, Bishop Barron observes, retains "the same basic spiritual maladjustment of seeking joy in some worldly object or set of values" rather than God himself.[22] Hence a man may love the law of God more than the God who gave the law. As a result, Barron observes, "The fussy moralist is often just the sensualist in a flimsy religious disguise."[23] Such a

19. Barron, *And Now I See*, 8.

20. McCormack, *A Guide to Formation Advising*, 117.

21. *Summa theologiae* 1-2.2. Cf. Robert Barron, *Seeds of the Word: Finding God in the Culture* (Skokie, IL: Word on Fire, 2015), 61.

22. Robert Barron, *The Priority of Christ: Toward a Postliberal Catholicism* (Grand Rapids, MI: Baker Academic, 2007), 87.

23. Barron, 87.

moralistic but fundamentally unconverted man is likely not fully aware of the contradiction between what he professes to believe and what he truly values. However, a combination of a structured prayer life, fraternal interactions with other men discerning the priesthood, and conversations with formators can be the means of encountering Jesus more deeply and discovering what areas of the seminarian's life the Lord is calling him to hand over.

If it turns out that the driving motivation for joining the seminary was something other than the Lord's call, the real act of *metanoia* for that man will be to leave the seminary and pursue his true vocation elsewhere. In saying this, I am not trying to imply that those who remain in the seminary are the truly converted, while those who leave are the worldly ones! Every man who enters is on a journey of self-discovery and greater conversion, of learning and experiencing that only God is the ultimate value, and of discerning how to live a life of habits and attitudes in keeping with that ultimate value. But even for those who discern a continuation of the path to priestly ministry, growth in self-awareness will enable them to better prepare for being conformed to Christ. It will lead to their interactions with their fellow seminarians, formators, and the people of God being "marked by a level of self-knowledge that permits ongoing growth, especially in his relationship with others."[24]

SELF-ACCEPTANCE

Right alongside growth in self-awareness is growth in self-acceptance. Although I am discussing them distinctly, they really go hand in hand, because a true Christian self-acceptance is accepting

24. *Program of Priestly Formation* 197.

the forgiveness of Jesus for our sinfulness and his proclamation that we are fundamentally good, made in the image and likeness of God. By the same token, the complete acknowledgment of one's sins and shortcomings can only become possible when one knows with confidence the love and affirmation of the Father that is deeper than our failings. Barron explains, "The proper starting point for any healthy Christian theological anthropology is a clear sense of the togetherness of original sin and likeness unto God." "For without the first, *metanoia* is unnecessary"—we would just accept our sinfulness as our true self, not see a need for change. "And without the second, it is impossible"—we would despair of overcoming our sinfulness and simply wallow in self-pity and/or self-indulgence. Barron concludes, "Thus, just as we must *look* at the dark face of our own sin, so we must look at the beauty that is God's enduring presence within us."[25]

In other words, even in the area of human formation, I would argue once again along with Barron that we need to look at the man ontologically and not be limited to partial views borrowed from secular science. In his book *The Strangest Way*, Barron suggests that the Christian path or "way" begins by finding our "center," the point from which all of our activity flows. That center, of course, is the love of God incarnate, Jesus Christ—as I'll discuss in the next chapter on spiritual formation. But from the point of view of theological anthropology, it is necessary for us to recognize one key fact—we are made in God's image and likeness. We bear the *imago Dei*, and it is this fact that needs to animate us as we grow in discovering who we are in the world. Barron writes, "This means that at the foundation of our existence, we are one with the divine power that continually

25. Barron, *And Now I See*, 6–7.

creates and sustains the universe; we are held and cherished by the infinite love of God. When we rest in this center and realize its power, we know that, in an ultimate sense, we are safe, or, in more classical religious language, 'saved.'"[26]

This is fundamentally a spiritual truth, but it has important psychological and emotional implications. A man does not need to spend himself hoping to earn the admiration and affirmation of the crowd, his family of origin, his peers, or even his formators. How many problems that arise in the course of formation and ministry can be avoided if this healing truth of the *imago Dei* penetrates a man's consciousness? Nor should a man approach his fellow seminarians or future parishioners as bit players or the supporting cast in the drama of his own heroic service of Christ. Each of them is made in the *imago Dei*, too, no matter what they say or do! If the seminarian accepts himself primarily for his fundamental gift of being a person made by God who has become a child of God through Baptism, then he is driven by simple logic to accept all other persons and especially the baptized as his equals. The ontological roots of the person as *imago Dei* lead to a combination of a deep sense of self-esteem and a profound sense of humility.

In this process of human formation, Deacon McCormack observes that there is an important role for "community life, ministry, and [the seminarian's] relationship to the formators, spiritual director, and formation advisor."[27] Living in close quarters with other men of differing backgrounds and opinions becomes a school of recognizing one's weaknesses and limitations and accepting differences within

26. Barron, xv.

27. McCormack, *A Guide to Formation Advising*, 11.

the unity of God's Church. Pope Benedict XVI wrote in his *Letter to Seminarians*, "The seminary is a time when you learn with one another and from one another. In community life, which can at times be difficult, you should learn generosity and tolerance, not only bearing with, but also enriching one another, so that each of you will be able to contribute his own gifts to the whole, even as all serve the same Church, the same Lord."[28]

By hearing the stories and different experiences of others, the seminarian comes to see himself more distinctly. Deacon McCormack observes that "integral growth" through the formation process requires the seminarian to come "to understand his story, his gifts, and his weaknesses while learning to integrate these under the influence of the Holy Spirit."[29] I think it is important to point out that knowing one's gifts, strengths, and weaknesses does not mean coming to identify oneself with them—the seminarian should not aspire to be the "smart priest" or the "cool priest," the "athlete priest" or the "chef priest." If those are part of his personality, great! But more fundamentally he should know that he is made in the image of God, just like everyone else. Nor should he run screaming from any psychological difficulties uncovered in this process; the Church brings professional services to bear as well as spiritual resources. Deacon McCormack observes that "for those dealing with problematic issues that stem from their family of origin or other life experiences, psychological counseling will be very beneficial."[30] Far from theological anthropology simply replacing more mundane

28. Benedict XVI, "Letter of His Holiness Benedict XVI to Seminarians" 7, October 18, 2010, vatican.va.

29. McCormack, *A Guide to Formation Advising*, 11.

30. McCormack, 11.

efforts at healing, it will make them more fruitful because it will give them the firmest foundation in a humble self-acceptance as the *imago Dei*.

SELF-MASTERY AND CELIBACY

The second stage of seminary formation is known as "the discipleship stage" and generally coincides with the study of philosophy. On the level of human formation, the *Program of Priestly Formation* refers to "the training of one's character in Christian virtue, so as to lay a solid foundation for future stages."[31] As I have repeated throughout this book, the old scholastic adage "You cannot give what you do not have" applies here: If the height of Christian virtue is self-gift, how can one give oneself without first possessing oneself? We call this disposition "self-mastery"—that is, mastery over one's actions and dispositions. Of course, training in self-mastery begins at the propaedeutic stage and continues in later stages of formation, but I would suggest that it is a special focus of this discipleship stage as a seminarian takes on full-time coursework and otherwise resumes a more "active" life after the relatively unencumbered time in the propaedeutic stage.

It would be a mistake to see this time of discipleship—paired as it is with the exploration of human reason (philosophy)—as a time to work on natural virtues, parallel to but separate from the focus of spiritual formation at this time ("growing in an intimate relationship with Jesus Christ").[32] As Barron observes, even in the area of personal virtue, Christianity is not a religion of heroic self-achievement but of

31. *Program of Priestly Formation* 132.

32. *Program of Priestly Formation* 132.

childlike receptivity to a divine gift: "We don't stand at the bottom of the holy mountain wondering whether we can clamber our way to the summit, attaining the divine through our heroic efforts. On the contrary, through God's grace, we start on the mountaintop, as the beloved children of God, cherished and redeemed."[33]

Therefore, as I have explained in a previous chapter, the Incarnation of Jesus is "*not something to be admired from the outside, but rather an energy in which to participate.*"[34] The seminarian will plug in to this energy through meditation and contemplation, and the privileged place for discussing this interior conversation with the Lord will be meeting with his spiritual director and other spiritual formation staff. But he will also be able to assess his visible progress in living in conformity with the Gospel through his meetings with his formation advisor and other human formation staff. While the confession of sins is as private for the seminarian as for any member of the faithful, it is imperative for his discernment and progress that the seminarian share any struggles with particular habits or areas of the moral life with his formation advisor and other members of the seminary community who would help him to grow and work on those issues. It may be in many cases that the underlying problem driving the behavior lies deeper and points back to growing further in self-knowledge and self-acceptance.

Of particular concern to the Church is formation in chastity for lifelong celibacy. Needless to say, this is an area in which a weakness or deficiency is of particular concern, as it can lead to scandal within priestly ministry or even the end of a priest's ministry. We saw

33. Robert Barron, *The Strangest Way: Walking the Christian Path* (Park Ridge, IL: Word on Fire Institute, 2021), 30–31.

34. Barron, *And Now I See*, 3.

in an earlier chapter that from his time as a young priest, Barron was concerned that celibacy be seen not as a mere requirement or practical expediency but as a sign of a great love. In a more recent essay on the topic of priestly formation, Barron reiterates that celibacy "is, above all, a mode of love and not a negation. Having said that, however, John Paul knows that the living out of celibate love depends upon a remarkable asceticism."[35]

It is a long tradition in the Church that asceticism in sexual matters goes hand-in-hand with those other ascetical pillars recommended particularly during Lent: fasting and almsgiving. In *The Strangest Way*, Barron recalls how the demon in C.S. Lewis' book *The Screwtape Letters* tries to tempt the believer to spiritualize his beliefs and shun any physical practices of devotion (rosary beads, pilgrimages, etc.). In response, Barron argues that "if the desire for the center, the passion for God, be awakened, the more immediately pressing desires must be muted, and this is the purpose of fasting in its various forms."[36] It may surprise those who have never been to a Catholic seminary, but fasting can sometimes be harder than you might think: the cafeteria is usually very well stocked! Feasting is an important part of seminary life, but so too is fasting when appropriate. We may not wish to imitate the sometimes harsh penances of centuries past, but it is incumbent upon us as formators and seminarians not to be unfaithful in the small matter of food, lest we fail in great matters like sexual pleasure or, for that matter, honors and wealth.[37] A mundane but still important part of human formation is an ongoing conversation about healthy eating, exercise,

35. Barron, *Renewing Our Hope*, 177.

36. Barron, *Strangest Way*, 66.

37. See Luke 16:10.

and other forms of balanced living. In fact, in my experience, I think we generally do a good job encouraging seminarians today to take good care of their bodies as well as their souls.

The Program of Priestly Formation also calls attention to preparation for "simplicity of life," observing that it is "particularly important in our own age when human needs and desires are so consciously manipulated and exploited." The reason it gives is interesting: "a consumer society often reduces people to things."[38] This, of course, is also what an unchaste, frequently pornographic society does in the area of sexuality: reduce persons to the level of things. The Church is not simply training priests to avoid excesses in any of these areas—sexuality, food, or possessions—to avoid scandal or prevent obstacles to priestly ministry. She is profoundly concerned about the interior attitude of her priests, their appreciation for the world, and especially their care of individual persons.

In sum, to quote John Paul II: "Freedom requires the person to be truly master of oneself, determined to fight and overcome the different forms of selfishness and individualism that threaten the life of each one, ready to open out to others, generous in dedication and service to one's neighbor."[39]

The goal of all this striving for greater Christian virtue is not the enjoyment of isolated success but the gift of oneself to the community.

SELF-GIFT

The third stage of seminary formation is known as the configuration stage, in which "the seminarian models his life on the self-donation

38. *Program of Priestly Formation* 217.

39. John Paul II, *Pastores Dabo Vobis* 44.

of Jesus Christ, Shepherd and Servant, as he prepares more immediately for Holy Orders."[40] Although this is not the final stage of priestly formation, it is the last to take place in the seminary and the culmination of discernment of a priestly vocation, ending with the ordination to the transitional diaconate. Such a man should be "an example for younger seminarians" who "exercises authority and leadership well among his peers."[41] As a seminary professor, I can attest that it's always a pleasure to see the maturation of the men who have been developing through their seminary years, even if it means they will soon leave the training ground and enter the "battlefield" of ministry.

The final stage prior to ordination to the priesthood is the vocation synthesis stage, which comes after the ordination to the diaconate and takes place in a ministry setting. The *Program of Priestly Formation* explains that "during this stage he works to overcome any human fears, and he grows in the freedom of natural self-confidence to be able to bring the Gospel to all those who need it."[42] The needs and challenges of the people of God today are daunting; it's one thing to talk about them within the seminary, which is intentionally a protected environment, but another thing to confront them face to face. To be the one to walk with a person in poverty and mental illness or to sit with a family grieving a loved one is something else entirely. It's natural to be afraid of falling short in our attempts to help and comfort them.

Robert Barron explains that "to overcome fear is to move from the *pusilla anima* (small soul) to the *magna anima* (great soul)."[43]

40. *Program of Priestly Formation* 135.

41. *Program of Priestly Formation* 198.

42. *Program of Priestly Formation* 200.

43. Barron, *And Now I See*, xv.

As I discussed in the last chapter, it is to develop the virtue of magnanimity (great-souledness)—not in the sense of lording one's new clerical state over others but in learning to be a servant to all (see Matt. 20:25–27). Therefore, the Church is wise to give men a time to exercise ministry as a deacon—that is, servant—because it is a time to develop this great-hearted attitude of service that must underlie their eventual priestly ministry. The deacon is a very specific kind of servant, as Bishop W. Shawn McKnight explains in his book *Understanding the Diaconate*: *diakonos* in Greek signified a "go-between," "one who acts at his master's bidding to convey messages and to perform tasks that require immediate attention, mobility, and speed,"[44] especially for the gods. The term could be used synonymously for ambassador. If you're an ambassador, it's not about you! (see 2 Cor. 5:20). Rather, you are respected because of the greatness of the one you represent, and it's clear that you're there to do what your superiors direct you to do (without grumbling!), not what you might think is best.

There are two ways that this service can be spoiled by fear. The most obviously fearful way is to do too little—to do only what is asked of you, with the excuse that you're only following orders—and to thus avoid putting your heart into the work. A good ambassador not only represents his master faithfully; he tries to win over the people to whom he's sent. But the more subtle temptation in response to fear is to do too much—that is, to cover up one's insecurities through overactivity, through trying to please or impress everyone. This can become a kind of grasping, in which "we see ourselves as

44. W. Shawn McKnight, *Understanding the Diaconate: Historical, Theological, and Sociological Foundations* (Washington, DC: The Catholic University of America Press, 2018), 6.

the threatened center of a hostile universe" and therefore think it is up to us to solve all the problems and right all the wrongs.[45] By contrast, Barron describes the *magna anima* as a soul that "neither grasps nor hides, but rather opens itself in awe and gratitude to the ever greater, ever more alluring Mystery."[46]

Hence, just as self-acceptance and self-mastery ultimately require a theological anthropology, so too a mature self-gift requires us to root our humanity in the divinity of Christ. Barron explains that living from fear is "a function of living our lives at the surface level, a result of forgetting our deepest identity."[47] A genuine magnanimity comes instead with self-confidence as a beloved Son of God as well as self-awareness regarding my own limitations and "appropriate boundaries" in ministerial relationships.[48] On the level of human formation, this means remembering that even in your service, you are a son of God called to the dignity of ministry, and therefore you need to maintain your own body, psyche, and spirit. You have to keep up the disciplines of prayer, rest, exercise, and study that you developed in the seminary environment. Being self-giving does not mean becoming self-destructive.

In other words, instead of seeking to fill all our time with tasks, we have to let the Lord fill us with his love. In his commentary on the Song of Songs, Bernard of Clairvaux has this insight:

> The man who is wise, therefore, will see his life as more like a reservoir than a canal. The canal simultaneously pours out what

45. Barron, *And Now I See*, xv.
46. Barron, 79.
47. Barron, xv.
48. *Program of Priestly Formation* 199.

> it receives; the reservoir retains the water till it is filled, then discharges the overflow without loss. . . . Today there are many in the Church who act like canals, the reservoirs are far too rare. So urgent is the charity of those through whom the streams of heavenly doctrine flow to us, that they want to pour it forth before they have been filled; they are more ready to speak than to listen, impatient to teach what they have not grasped, and full of presumption to govern others while they know not how to govern themselves.[49]

The vocational synthesis stage is thus a time for patience as well as courage. It is a time to begin to teach, to speak, to pour forth, but even more, it is still part of formation—a time to listen, to learn, to be governed rather than to govern. Barron observes that "a virtue such as courage really becomes intelligible only in the measure that it is displayed biographically."[50] In other words, you have to look at the well-lived Christian life as it is actually lived, not just as a set of guidelines or theories. This means learning from your own life experience, and from the wisdom of fellow priests and deacons as well as the faithful. But I also recommend this stage as a time to pay particular attention to the teachings and the biographies of the saints and other great figures in the history of the Church. You can learn many things from them, but above all, you can take courage in the splendor of their ultimate victory of faith. They now make up a "great . . . cloud of witnesses" accompanying you as you learn to serve not from a place of fear, but in awe of the Mystery by whom you've been called (Heb. 12:1).

49. Bernard of Clairvaux, *On the Song of Songs*, vol. 1, trans. Kilian J. Walsh (Kalamazoo, MI: Cistercian, 1971), 134.

50. Barron, *Priority of Christ*, 282.

THE KEY TO HUMAN FORMATION

I want to conclude by emphasizing a point that has been implicit throughout: all human formation is really self-formation. The *Program of Priestly Formation* says as much: "Seminarians bear the primary responsibility for their human formation. The role of the seminary is to assist them in achieving the integral human maturity."[51] This should be evident from the fact that human formation culminates in self-gift, and no institution or program can make a man give truly of himself. What we as seminary formators and supportive fellow Catholics can do is offer him the tools and the tried-and-true techniques to grow in self-awareness, self-acceptance, and self-mastery. We can point to the dangers of unchecked media usage, unhealthy habits, or unexamined psychological issues. We can discuss how to overcome biases and racial prejudices; how to foster rich friendships; how to maintain a healthy celibate sexuality. We can hold him accountable to the goals appropriate to his chosen vocation. But it is he himself who must do all these things. Only he can give his yes.

Nor can we give him a vocation to the priesthood; we can confirm his call on behalf of the Church, but only Christ can call him to this ministry. Only Christ can be the fulfillment of his human desires for truth, beauty, goodness, and unity. This is why he will need more than human formation; he will need spiritual formation. As Barron observes,

> Christianity is, first and foremost, a religion of the concrete and not the abstract. It takes its power not from a general religious consciousness, not from an ethical conviction, not from a

51. *Program of Priestly Formation* 206.

comfortable abstraction, but from the person Jesus Christ. It is Christ—in his uncompromising call to repentance, his unforgettable gestures of healing, his unique and disturbing praxis of forgiveness, his provocative nonviolence and especially his movement from godforsakenness and death to shalom-radiating Resurrection—that moves the believer to change of life and gift of self.[52]

52. Barron, *Bridging the Great Divide*, 19–20.

CHAPTER 5

The Spiritual Dimension

In the introduction to this book, I observed that "a priest must be a priest above all else"—that is, above every title or activity or source of identity. I then explained the crisis of identity in the priesthood and set about, for the remainder of part 1, to explain priestly identity using the theology of Bishop Barron as a key to help unlock the Church's rich teaching. The goal of all this theological investigation is so that we priests can "go set the world ablaze" in response to Jesus' call to mission. Yet to quote again that great scholastic axiom, "You cannot give what you do not have." By the grace of the priesthood, we can spread the fire of God's love to his people through the objective grace of the sacraments, but the fire will spread more rapidly if our own hearts are ablaze. To keep that fire alive, the life of prayer has to be central to the life of a priest. With our minds, we can see and understand who we should be; with our wills, we can desire and pursue our goals; but only with the Lord's help can we do it rightly.

The US bishops' *Program of Priestly Formation* puts this point front and center in its section on spiritual formation: "Those who aspire to be sent on mission, as the Apostles were, must first acquire the listening and learning heart of disciples."[1] This is true for every Christian who accepts the Lord's call of discipleship, whatever their state in life. Yet, the *Program* continues, "the spirituality cultivated in the seminary is specifically priestly."[2] Pope St. John Paul II describes the rationale of the spiritual formation of a priest in *Pastores Dabo Vobis*: "Just as for all the faithful spiritual formation is central and unifies their being and living as Christians, that is, as new creatures in Christ who walk in the Spirit, so too for every priest his spiritual formation is the core which unifies and gives life to his *being* a priest and his *acting* as a priest."[3]

All spiritual formation for prospective priests is based in the experience of being beloved sons of the Father. With all the faithful, they are incorporated into Christ's life by Baptism, sharing in the Lord's life as priest, prophet, and king, but as discussed in chapter 1, once they receive the sacrament of Holy Orders, priests "are configured to Christ, Head and Shepherd of the Church, our great high Priest."[4] It is not enough for priests just to agree to the tenets of the Church or to try to meet people's expectations of a Christian leader; the US bishops state that "spiritual formation is about forming the heart so that it will interiorize the sentiments and ways of acting of Jesus Christ, the Son of the Father, who always acted in communion with the Holy Spirit."[5] To reach this lofty goal, the priest must have a healthy prayer life, an ongoing relationship of open communication,

1. *Program of Priestly Formation* 226, 6th ed. (Washington, DC: United States Conference of Catholic Bishops, 2022).

2. *Program of Priestly Formation* 228.

3. John Paul II, *Pastores Dabo Vobis* 45, apostolic exhortation, March 25, 1992, vatican.va.

4. *Program of Priestly Formation* 228.

5. *Program of Priestly Formation* 228.

talking and listening to the Lord. This should already be flourishing by his final years in the seminary. In his seminary formation, a candidate for the priesthood learns the way of prayer, something that has to be as essential to him as breathing.

That being said, it's clear that due to original sin and the wounding of our nature, prayer is nowhere near as simple or natural to us as breathing, at least until we've gone through a great deal of training, purification, and healing. The *Program of Priestly Formation* lists no fewer than nineteen dimensions of spiritual formation for seminarians, of which I particularly wish to discuss the "four legs of the chair" I mentioned in chapter 3, which I take to be foundational for all the others: Eucharistic Adoration, spiritual reading, Marian devotion, and the Liturgy of the Hours.[6] Of course, in such a short chapter, I can only offer a few remarks to help orient the reader on a topic as rich as prayer, but that's okay! One of the beauties of spiritual formation in the seminary is that men are not left to read books and discern spirits by their own devices, but instead they are furnished with both a supportive community and an individual spiritual director who meets with them frequently.[7]

In pursuing this topic, I again want to follow a path laid out by Robert Barron. In his books *The Strangest Way: Walking the Christian Path* and *To Light a Fire on the Earth*, we learn three important essentials for the Christian spiritual life. The first thing is "to find the center"; the second is "to know you're a sinner"; and the third is to

6. These are Eucharist, Penance, Liturgy of the Hours, spiritual direction, Bible, retreats/days of recollection, personal meditation, the Fathers of the Church, devotions (especially Marian), apostolic service, asceticism, obedience, celibacy, simplicity, reconciliation, solidarity, solitude, discernment, and ongoing spiritual formation (*Program of Priestly Formation* 229).

7. *Program of Priestly Formation* 229 calls for biweekly meetings for spiritual direction.

recognize that "your life is not about you."[8] In this chapter, I would like to explain the life of prayer through these three essential aspects of following what Barron describes as "the strangest path." He used these insights in the spiritual formation of the seminarians entrusted to him as rector of Mundelein Seminary. He states that these three stages or aspects of growth are not his own invention but "are based on wisdom from the saints."[9] It is precisely this "strangest path" that might prove to be a helpful guide to the spiritual formation of the candidate for the priesthood.

FIND THE CENTER

First, Barron urges us to "find the center." What does he mean by this? I think it can be best explained by contrasting it with what it's like to be without a center. Martha, for instance, is gently rebuked by Jesus for being "worried and distracted by many things" (Luke 10:41). Martha's problem, on Barron's reading, is that "her mind, quite obviously, is divided, drifting from this concern to that, from one anxiety to another; there are *many things* that preoccupy her."[10] This is one way of being "uncentered." Another is found in the demoniacs of the Gospel of Mark, who speak "in the voice of the many, for the demonic consciousness is split, riven, uncentered." By contrast, the truly centered person's "entire life, in all of its multifacetedness, circles like a vortex around one center of gravity."[11] To live from the true center is to "breathe the air of real spiritual freedom,"

8. Robert Barron with John L. Allen Jr., *To Light a Fire on the Earth: Proclaiming the Gospel in a Secular Age* (New York: Image Books, 2017), 158–164, and Robert Barron, *The Strangest Way: Walking the Christian Path* (Park Ridge, IL: Word on Fire Institute, 2021).

9. Barron with Allen Jr., *To Light a Fire*, 158.

10. Barron, *Strangest Way*, 33.

11. Barron, 34.

to find a "shelter from the storm, a sure place to stand even as the chaos of sin crashes around us."[12]

In an article in *Chicago Catholic*, Barron further elaborates on this notion of the center, in which he turns, as he so often does, to literature. Specifically, he describes a spiritual classic, *The Way of the Pilgrim*, written by an anonymous Russian Orthodox Christian about a pilgrim who tries to live out St. Paul's admonition from his First Letter to the Thessalonians to "pray without ceasing" (1 Thess. 5:17). How can that be done in the contemporary world, which is beset by all the business and burdens of modern life? The pilgrim learns to pray a simple prayer constantly, the famous "Jesus Prayer." As one breathes in, one says, "Lord Jesus Christ," and as one breathes out, one says, "have mercy on me." In the course of his journey, the pilgrim has only two prized possessions—his Bible and his prayer book, the *Philokalia*—and both are taken from him. Eventually, he is able to reclaim his books. Barron writes:

> Through a fortuitous set of circumstances, he managed to recover his lost possessions, and when he had them once again, he hugged them to his chest, gripping them so hard that his fingers practically locked in place around them.
>
> I would invite you to stay with that image for a moment. We see a man with no wealth, no power, no influence in society, no fame to speak of, practically no physical possessions—but clinging with all of his might and with fierce protectiveness to two things whose sole purpose is to feed his soul.

12. Barron, 45, 47.

Here's my question for you: What would you cling to in such a way? What precisely is it, the loss of which would produce in you a kind of panic? What would make you cry, once you realized that you no longer had it? And to make the questions more pointed, let's assume that you were on a desert island or that you, like the Russian pilgrim, had no resources to go out and buy a replacement. Would it be your car? Your home? Your golf clubs? Your computer?

To be honest, I think for me it might be my iPhone. If suddenly I lost my ability to make a call, my contacts, my music, my GPS, my maps, my email, etc., I would panic—and I would probably cry for sheer joy once I had the phone back, and my fingers would close around it like a claw. What makes this confession more than a little troubling is that, 10 years ago, I didn't even own a cell phone. I lived my life perfectly well without it, and if you had told me then that I would never have one, it wouldn't have bothered me a bit.

What I particularly love about the pilgrim is that he was preoccupied, not about any of the passing, evanescent goods of the world, but rather about prayer, about a sustained contact with the eternal God. He didn't care about the things that obsess most of us most of the time: money, power, fame, success. The only possessions that concerned him were those simple books that fed his relationship to God. Or to turn it around, he wasn't frightened by the loss of any finite good; but he was frightened to death at the prospect of losing his contact with the living God.

> What would you cling to like a desperate animal? What loss would you fear? What do you ultimately love?[13]

As anyone who grew up in Catholic school or religious education could tell you, the correct answer to this question is Jesus. He alone must be our center. Our relationship with him—our Lord and God, our Savior and brother—must be our "area of ultimate concern." The *Program of Priestly Formation* lays down the core of spiritual formation rather simply: "The basic principle of spiritual formation is expressed in *Pastores Dabo Vobis* [45] and is a synthesis of the teachings of *Optatam Totius*: The seminarian is called 'to live in intimate and unceasing union with God the Father through his Son Jesus Christ, in the Holy Spirit.'"[14]

But the challenge put forward by Barron's image of the pilgrim is this: How can Jesus become for us the subject of such intense reliance, such clinging and dependent love, much like the love of a small child for its parents (see Matt. 18:3)?

Bishop Barron acknowledges at the start of *The Strangest Way* that we often don't start out by wanting to be such needy or even desperate lovers of Christ. We think instead that we have to work very hard or try many spiritual disciplines before we can be worthy of real relationship with him. Barron observes, "Deep down, many of us Christians still believe that God is a rivalrous Lord who dispenses favors grudgingly, only after a demonstration of virtue

13. Bishop Robert Barron, "A Pilgrim, a Bishop and an iPhone," *Chicago Catholic*, December 11, 2016, https://www.chicagocatholic.com/bishop-robert-barron/-/article/2016/12/11/a-pilgrim-a-bishop-and-an-ipho-2.

14. *Program of Priestly Formation* 226.

on our part."[15] But contrary to this "Promethean temptation," the "new center comes to us as a divine gift, and our first responsibility is to welcome it."[16]

In other words, we do not need to climb a high mountaintop to reach an experience of the divine. That is because God has come down to us and has become one of us. As St. Paul says, "Do not say in your heart, 'Who will ascend into heaven?' . . . The word is near you, on your lips and in your heart" (Rom. 10:6, 8). We recognize God's closeness to us in the Gospels, especially the story of Christmas. Still, we might feel that after his Resurrection and Ascension, he has left us again so that we have to grapple once more with the problem of how to make tangible in our lives this mystery of the Incarnation and of God's presence in our lives. Many of our men entering the seminary have a strong sense that God is an abstraction, that we are distant from him and he from us. This is not only the lot of terrible sinners or demoniacs (who would be screened out by the psychological testing anyway); plenty of good Catholic men are, like Martha, friends of the Lord who nevertheless don't yet feel the "real spiritual freedom" or "shelter from the storm" that Jesus promises to be.

Thankfully, Jesus already foresaw and solved this problem. In fact, for men in the seminary and most Catholics who might read this book, the solution is literally handed to them every week, if not every day. And that solution is the Eucharist!

The Eucharist is "the source and summit of the Christian life," as Vatican II affirms and the *Program of Priestly Formation* reiterates,

15. Barron, *Strangest Way*, 31.

16. Barron, 30.

precisely because it is the privileged place in which Christ manifests himself to us and draws us into our center.[17] Because Christ makes himself available to us as food and drink, he enables us to hunger and thirst to receive him in a way that will bring into harmony our spirit, soul, and body. Barron shares a marvelous experience of seeing this spiritual hunger among the faithful in his book on the Eucharist:

> In the Spring of 2007, I was privileged to be a scholar in residence at the North American College in Rome. During that period, I had the opportunity, on three occasions, to distribute communion at Mass in St. Peter's Square. Standing on one side of a partition, I watched as scores of people came forward to receive the Eucharist. In the typically Italian style, things were a tad disorganized, and the faithful were compelled, in the press of the crowd, to stretch out their hands toward me. I saw all sorts of hands—old and young, dirty and clean, lined and unlined—reaching out for the Bread of Life. When I would move along the partition, some would cry out to me plaintively, "Padre, Padre, per favore" (Father, Father, please). Never before in my priesthood, though I had distributed communion to thousands, had I had the sense of carrying food to those who were desperate for it. Those faithful in St. Peter's Square embodied a truth that is deep in our Catholic tradition, though too infrequently stated: the Eucharist is not a luxury but a necessity, for without it we would, in the spiritual sense, starve to death.[18]

17. *Program of Priestly Formation* 229; see *Catechism of the Catholic Church* 1324 (cf. *Lumen Gentium* 11).

18. Robert Barron, *Eucharist* (Park Ridge, IL: Word on Fire Institute, [2008] 2021), 1.

For whom were the people clamoring? Christ himself. And to whom were they clamoring? Padre, padre . . . the priest—not because Barron was a brilliant academic or even a man of holiness, but simply because he had accepted the call of God to stand *in persona Christi* and share this precious gift of the Eucharist—this "one thing necessary"—with God's people.

This is the great call to which we priests are responding, the great need for which God is sending us. When people ask us—as they inevitably will—why we would even consider becoming a priest in today's world, this is the answer. Why would we leave behind family and wealth and freedom to serve in such a maligned and sometimes dysfunctional organization as the Catholic Church? The Eucharist is the answer: nowhere else in the history of the universe has the divine center come so close to us mortal beings; nowhere else in the world do we touch and taste the answer to the question that is every life.[19] Priestly spirituality is, first and foremost, Eucharistic spirituality. The Eucharistic Lord is the one to whom we cling, the one whose loss we most fear.

Spiritual formation in the seminary is not about increasing the graces available to us in the Eucharist; we already receive, at every Mass, the complete gift: Jesus Christ, Body, Blood, Soul, and Divinity. Rather, it is about increasing our receptivity to those graces, which begins by actually encouraging our hunger for his Sacred Body and learning to recognize our own thirst as a thirst for his Precious Blood. One of the primary ways—outside of the Mass itself—that we increase our spiritual hunger, in my experience, is

19. See John Paul II, "Homily at Oriole Park at Camden Yards, Baltimore," October 8, 1995, vatican.va.

by spending time in Adoration of the Blessed Sacrament. Barron recommends the practice of a daily "Holy Hour" of prayer in the presence of the Eucharistic Lord. This was not something that was a part of his own seminary formation, but he learned of its value from his seminarians at Mundelein.[20]

Barron says that the most important part of the Holy Hour is showing up; there are many ways to structure that time, but to "take the time" is the nonnegotiable necessity.[21] Barron's general recommendations for ways to spend the Holy Hour include all the basic kinds of prayer outlined in the *Catechism of the Catholic Church*: blessing and adoration, obviously, but also petition and contrition, intercession, thanksgiving, and praise.[22] He himself often starts with the Rosary or by repeating the Jesus Prayer, going on to pray the Liturgy of the Hours, and concluding with some time of silent meditation. He also usually has a book of spiritual reading at hand—which is to say, in this one hour he might do everything that I say in this chapter is most essential to the priest's spiritual life!

In the middle of the Holy Hour, Barron also tries to leave some time just to be with the Lord. For him, prayer is, ultimately, "a conversation between friends. . . . It's our friendship with God, expressed in this lively conversation."[23] He advises us in this conversational prayer to "speak with honesty," to avoid only a recitation of "a bunch of pious language."[24] God already knows us each inside

20. "355: How to Make a Holy Hour," *Word on Fire Show* podcast, October 10, 2022, https://www.wordonfire.org/videos/wordonfire-show/episode355/. Barron identifies Archbishop Fulton Sheen (1895–1979) as a great promoter of this practice.

21. Barron with Allen Jr., *To Light a Fire*, 143.

22. *Catechism of the Catholic Church* 2626–2643.

23. Barron with Allen Jr., *To Light a Fire*, 140.

24. Barron with Allen Jr., 142.

and out. Barron also encourages us to "listen attentively," making sure it is not only us talking, but that we listen to how God speaks to us through Scripture and in silence. Finally, he suggests, "work on the silent savoring."[25]

At times, spending an hour in the presence of the Eucharistic Lord is full of delight; at other times, we are like the disciples in the boats tossed about the sea, the waves being "failure, sickness, anxiety, depression, the attacks of our enemies, the fear of death itself."[26] So long as we continue to stay near him, even these difficult times will increase our hunger and thirst, and therefore confirm again and again that he is our center and our Savior.

KNOW YOU'RE A SINNER

The second path that Barron describes in *The Strangest Way* is to know that you're a sinner. This aspect of Christian life follows closely from the first, for, as Barron observes, "the center is not only alluring; it is also demanding, for it has not only the soft edge of beauty but the hard edge of truth."[27] He cites both Isaiah from the Old Testament and Simon Peter from the New Testament as men who respond to the presence of the Lord not with delight but with an awe-filled awareness of their complete unworthiness. In fact, each of them tells the divine in their midst to "go away," because they do not think that they can measure up to the task asked of them.[28]

In a sense, they are right! Isaiah is not good enough when he is called to be a prophet, nor Simon Peter to be an Apostle, let alone

25. Barron with Allen Jr., 144.

26. Barron, *Strangest Way*, 48.

27. Barron, 39.

28. Barron, 72, citing Isaiah 6:5 and Luke 5:8.

the head of the Church! Yet in neither case does God let them off the hook so easily. Their awe is understandable, but their feeble attempts to get rid of God are never commended. While they are in one sense humble, I think each man's proclamation of unworthiness shares in the "Promethean" temptation that Barron had discussed before—they want God to come to them only when they are ready, when their ducks are all in a row. I see the same problem sometimes in men deciding whether to enter the seminary: "Do I really have what it takes?"

I want to reassure them: you don't have to have what it takes to be a priest when you begin the journey to ordination! If you have those basic characteristics of every good seminarian that I described in chapter 1, there's no reason to wait any longer to begin discerning your vocation.[29] Being a priest is indeed a call to an elite ministry, which includes being a prophet and an apostle, but there's a reason why we put men through eight years of formation: they aren't ready to be priests when they start! Simon didn't have what it took when he was called—neither did Isaiah. That's why in each case, it was God who said, "Don't worry, I got this." He touched Isaiah's lips with a burning coal to make him pure enough to preach God's word; he gave Simon a new name and promised, "I will make you a fisher of men." In both cases, no matter how unworthy they felt, they had the humility to say yes to God. They let go of the Promethean temptation and allowed themselves to be formed and led.

Now, it's also true, as I discussed in the last chapter, that there are certain basic human foundations without which a man cannot

29. As a reminder, these are the four basic characteristics: first, an openness to the workings of the Lord; second, a prayerful spirit; third, an openness to growing in the intellectual understanding of the faith; and fourth, a desire to serve.

become a good priest.[30] We look for these when we decide to accept a man into seminary, and we keep looking as we decide whether to recommend that he continue advancing toward the priesthood. If one or more of those are missing—which is no shame—we will let a man know that he is not a suitable candidate for the priesthood.[31] Or if some sinful or bad habit poses a continuing threat to a man's potential ministry—particularly in regard to sexuality, money, or obedience—we have ways of identifying and addressing these concerns. But that external role of discernment by the seminary and diocese should give the man all the more assurance to follow what he senses the Lord's call to be. Instead of asking the Lord to leave him, he should pray, "God, be merciful to me, a sinner," like the tax collector of Luke 18:13.

I find a lot of earnest young Catholic men who do see themselves as the tax collector of Luke 18:13, saying, "Be merciful to me." They frequent the sacrament of Confession, learn all the teachings of the Church eagerly, and strive for holiness. But they still—despite the Lord's warning—aspire to become the Pharisee of the same parable, who can stand in front of others saying to himself, "God, I thank you that I am not like other people" (Luke 18:11).[32] In other words, they see being a sinner as something to grow out of, and they can become exasperated at times by their slow progress toward perfection. Sadly, they can also become exasperated or even scandalized by the leaders

30. And there are formal requirements of canon law; see Code of Canon Law 1026–1052, vatican.va.

31. Of course, there are stories of saints like St. John Vianney or St. Joseph of Cupertino, who, in the course of their studies, were denied progression due to an academic inaptitude, but who ultimately attained the priesthood and flourished. I don't mean to suggest that seminary formators are infallible, but we do our best.

32. See Barron, *Strangest Way*, 76.

of the Church—including their seminary leaders—because they expect perfection from them as well.

Barron, by contrast, assures us that we will always be sinners on this earth. Sin cannot be fully vanquished in this life—and accepting this is a key to sanctity. He uses the example of that Pharisee of Pharisees, St. Paul. "Saul of Tarsus galloped off to Damascus to persecute the Church of Christ, utterly convinced that he was following the will of God." Before he was struck by the divine voice and light, Saul had "focus, energy, and aggressive confidence. But in the wake of the shock of the light, he lies on the ground, eyes shut, arms groping into the darkness, his confidence dissipated. And it is at this moment that he begins to be a saint."[33] Learning to follow the will of God brought him a boundless new confidence to preach the Gospel, but it never removed the tension within him between grace and sin. Even twenty years after his conversion, he wrote to the Romans, "For I do not do what I want, but I do the very thing I hate" (Rom. 7:15). He told the Corinthians that he begged God to take away a particular struggle, but the Lord only responded, "My grace is sufficient for you, for power is made perfect in weakness" (2 Cor. 12:9). In the First Letter to Timothy, Paul wrote that he is "the foremost" of sinners (1 Tim. 1:15)—not in the past tense but the present.

Barron is surely not trying to encourage us to despair of God's mercy, the forgiveness of sins, or the call to sanctity. Indeed, he writes in *Vibrant Paradoxes*, "The Church calls people to be not spiritual mediocrities, but great saints, and this is why its moral ideals are so stringent. Yet the Church also mediates the infinite

33. Barron, *Strangest Way*, 73.

mercy of God to those who fail to live up to that ideal (which means practically everyone). This is why its forgiveness is so generous and so absolute. To grasp both of these extremes is to understand the Catholic approach to morality."[34]

The saints, he says, do not continue to call themselves sinners out of a false humility, but because they grasp these extremes. They are not comparing themselves to other people (like the Pharisee in the parable does)—they are comparing themselves to God. Barron uses an analogy from his experience:

> In Chicago during the wintertime, tons of salt are dumped on the roadways to keep them clear of ice and snow, but then that salt is kicked up onto cars and windshields. When one is driving at night, away from direct lighting, one can see fairly well, even through a salt-caked windshield. But come the next morning, when one is driving straight toward the rising sun, that same windshield is suddenly opaque. John of the Cross said that the soul is like a pane of glass and God's love is like the sun. It is, accordingly, when God's love is shining most directly on the soul that its smudges and imperfections are most apparent.[35]

True humility does not come from putting ourselves down, but rather from letting the light of the Lord's face shine upon us (see Num. 6:25; Ps. 67:2).

34. Robert Barron, *Vibrant Paradoxes: The Both/And of Catholicism* (Skokie, IL: Word on Fire, 2016), 7.

35. Barron, *Strangest Way*, 72. See John of the Cross, *The Dark Night*, in *The Collected Works of St. John of the Cross*, trans. Kieran Kavanaugh and Otilio Rodriguez (Washington, DC: ICS, 1979), 344.

There are many aspects of seminary life that shine this light: encountering the sacraments, especially Confession; interactions with one's peers; the work of formators. But I want to highlight two especially: spiritual reading (particularly meditation on Scripture) and Marian devotion (particularly the Rosary). The Letter to the Hebrews recommends looking to Scripture because "the word of God is living and active, sharper than any two-edged sword, piercing until it divides soul from spirit, joints from marrow; it is able to judge the thoughts and intentions of the heart" (Heb. 4:12). If we have a tendency like the Pharisee to pat ourselves on the back, the parable about him will bring us up short. If we are too busy with activity and lose our contemplation, we can be cut to the heart by the story of Mary and Martha and "the one thing necessary." And so on.

We hear these Gospels and the whole of the Scriptures through the liturgy, and that is the natural place for them, but it's important not just to stop there. If the first fundamental rule of the spiritual life is "take the time," we have to take the time to meditate and reflect on these passages, to allow them to sink in and to honestly assess whether we live according to them and how they call us to a greater repentance and belief in the Gospel. Other spiritual reading is, at its best, just another way of meditating upon the Scriptures. After all, the Bible is reflected and magnified and illuminated in the writings of the Fathers of the Church all the way up through the popes and theologians of today. These authors can give us a much clearer idea of how to apply the words of Scripture to ourselves—especially the often-murky Old Testament. Barron does this throughout his works,[36] even as he also draws connections to great literature and popular culture.

By contrast, I would warn young men interested in the priesthood not to spend too much time with "spiritual" writers who get too far away from the Scriptures. As priests, the fruits of their contemplation will often become the fodder for preaching, and this preaching should be of the Gospel of Christ and not a gospel of self-help. Nor is spiritual reading a time for intellectual study, for just learning things about the Lord, as important as that is. The two are very connected—good theology leads to good spirituality, and Scripture is the soul of theology—but spiritual reading is specifically for allowing those truths to penetrate one's heart, not to prepare for a test. To give one indication of the difference, in spiritual reading, one should stop whenever an insight leads to prayer, whereas if a man is doing the readings for his next class with me, I want him to finish them all!

Second, I always encourage my seminarians not to become so busy that they neglect devotion to Our Lady. Mary is "the model of a faith that is consistently and seriously *quaerens intellectum* (seeking understanding)," Barron writes, by "treasuring the events of salvation history in her heart."[37] To pray the Rosary consistently is to be drawn with Mary particularly into the events of the life of Jesus, to recall his humanity, how he grew and suffered—like us in all things but sin. I don't say that everyone has to pray the Rosary, but it is the Marian devotion that I most recommend for priests. It was fashionable for a

36. See, for instance, his application of the story of the prophet Samuel and the priest Eli to the sexual abuse crisis in the Church in *Renewing Our Hope: Essays for the New Evangelization* (Washington, DC: The Catholic University of America Press, 2020), 155–157.

37. Barron, *Renewing Our Hope*, 26. Barron is describing specifically the Mariology of St. John Henry Newman in this passage.

while to shun the Rosary as too lowbrow for intellectual Christians, but thankfully I think that has changed when you see someone as intellectual as Bishop Barron promoting it.[38]

In our Protestant culture in America, it's easy to be hesitant about Marian devotion, to worry that having a relationship with her might detract from our relationship with God. If we have Jesus, why do we need Mary? I respond that it's always interesting to meet the parents of my seminarians, especially their mothers, because it gives such a window into their personalities. The same is true for our mother Mary and her son Jesus. But more importantly, she is also our mother, too, given to us by Jesus at the foot of the cross on account of her faith; she is there for us especially when we feel forsaken by God or have difficulty approaching him for some reason.[39]

Of course, praying the Rosary helps us know that we're sinners. After all, while praying it, you say 50 or 150 times, "pray for us sinners." But even more importantly, the Rosary reminds us that at the center of our faith is not a set of rules or virtues but, as Pope Benedict wrote, "the encounter with an event, a person, which gives life a new horizon and a decisive direction."[40] The problem of perfectionism—of hoping to outgrow being a sinner before we enter into heaven—comes from forgetting that being a Christian is all about relationship. When we become too puffed up or too discouraged, the humility of Mary—the only actually sinless one

38. In *To Light a Fire*, Barron mentions a lesson learned from observing his doctoral director at the Institut Catholique in Paris, Fr. Michel Corbin, before a seminar class. "There's Corbin, by himself, and he has a rosary in his right hand," Barron recalls. "I kind of surprised him, and I thought, Wow, here's a French professor of theology praying the rosary. Corbin really helped me to see the liturgical and spiritual and prayerful dimension of what we were doing. I think that opened a door that I went through" (141).

39. John 19:26–27. See Cardinal Raniero Cantalamessa, *The Power of the Cross: Good Friday Sermons from the Papal Preacher* (Elk Grove Village, IL: Word on Fire, 2023), 82–83.

40. Benedict XVI, *Deus Caritas Est* 1, encyclical letter, December 25, 2005, vatican.va.

apart from Christ—brings us back to that relationship and shows us how to live it: magnifying the Lord.

IT'S NOT ABOUT YOU!

The problem of sin and the need for grace has been true throughout human history, but there are special aspects of the modern world that are different from previous eras. Barron is acutely aware of one of the greatest problems of modernity: the fractured self. Caught in the belief of a mind-body split articulated by René Descartes,[41] we have seen Christianity go from a "sacred way, expressed in movement, practice and apprenticeship" to a "faint echo of the secular culture or a privatized and individualized set of convictions."[42] Bishop Barron describes this as a "beige, bland, attenuated Christianity,"[43] which is no match for the modern world of subjectivity. We are all affected by the Cartesian approach to reality, one which is "subjectivist, rationalist, suspicious,"[44] including in the manner in which we approach religion.

Theology has not been immune to these approaches. Barron cites two theologians who exercised tremendous influence at the time of his seminary formation: Karl Rahner, a Catholic, and Paul Tillich, a Protestant. Despite all that can be learned from their theologies, he sees them as influenced by two Germans of the eighteenth and early-nineteenth centuries: the philosopher Immanuel Kant and the theologian Friedrich Schleiermacher. These thinkers were trying to

41. René Descartes (1596–1650) was a French philosopher famous for his dualistic view of the mind and body.

42. Barron, *Strangest Way*, 13.

43. Barron, 14.

44. Barron, 15.

find a place for faith in the new intellectual climate of the modern world, but they replaced the objectivity of ontological Christianity with a more subjective approach. Barron describes their approach in these terms: "Interior, subjective experience is the religious *terra firma*, the rock upon which the whole structure is built."[45]

By contrast, Barron teaches repeatedly, "It's not about you." In many ways, adulthood is about triumphing over our own selfishness. I often think of parents who make such tremendous sacrifices for their children, forgoing their own individual pleasures and preferences to care for a sick child or to offer their child the finest education that one could receive. I think of my own parents, who struggled and saved to put me, my brother, and my sisters through a quality Catholic education. As mature Christians, our lives are not about us: they are about the Lord and those we have been blessed to have in our lives. Barron says, "Holy people are those who realize that they participate in something and Someone infinitely greater than themselves, that they are but fragments of Reality. . . . Far from crushing them, this awareness makes them great, capacious, whole."[46] To use a phrase from Balthasar, it is a growing movement from an "ego-drama" to a "theo-drama."[47] Barron writes, "Of course, our dramas are always uninteresting, even if we are playing the lead role. The key is to find the role that God has designed for us, even if it looks like a bit part."[48] When we accept this role, we find "there is a Power that is operative in us and accompanies us whether we

45. Barron, 16.

46. Barron with Allen Jr., *To Light a Fire*, 162.

47. Barron with Allen Jr., 163.

48. Barron with Allen Jr., 163.

know it or not and that will accomplish what we, by our own power, could never accomplish."[49]

This is true for all Christians, but how much more for priests! Priestly identity is all about being conformed to Christ so as to be able to act *in persona Christi* in a way that totally surpasses our own abilities. Barron writes, "On the third path, we are sent to do the work of Jesus, perhaps even to do 'greater works' than he himself (John 14:12)."[50] Nowhere is this more evident than in the Eucharist. At the Mass, on that altar, heaven and earth kiss, and we are transformed! When we gather for Mass, we are involved in the greatest adventure this side of heaven.

It is obvious that the priest is not ordained so that he can consecrate the Eucharist for himself. As a priest, I recognize that my closeness to the Eucharistic Lord—as much as I may treasure it—is not about me! I have been given this closeness with the Lord in the Eucharist precisely so that I can give him away to others. Thinking about the chalice that was passed down to me at my ordination helps remind me of this sacred trust. The Eucharist is not simply a means of connecting me personally to God through Christ; it also intrinsically draws me together with the community.

There is a debate that goes back and forth among certain theologians: Should we stop focusing on the Eucharist as the one, single sacrifice of Christ on the cross and instead say that the Eucharist is a coming together of the Church in thanksgiving and fellowship? According to Barron, we should not overemphasize either of these aspects so as to deny the other. It is a both/and rather than an

49. Barron, *Strangest Way*, 126.
50. Barron, 126.

either/or. If we lose the metaphysical aspects of the Eucharistic celebration—if we deny the Real Presence of Jesus in the Eucharist or the connection to the sacrifice of Calvary—then we become trapped in the immanent frame of modernity. On this scenario, we gather together as a community but become unreceptive to heavenly graces. But if we lose the communal aspects of the Eucharistic celebration, then we cannot free ourselves from the individualism of modern religion, even while physically sharing the same building. Barron observes, "The Neoplatonist philosopher Plotinus summed up the spiritual life in the phrase to be alone with the Alone."[51] This is not Christianity. Barron continues, "Plotinian devotees would certainly agree that their lives are not about them, but they would have no sense of being *sent* anywhere by the Alone. There is not the slightest trace of this self-absorbed mysticism in the biblical tradition. No one in the Bible is ever given an experience of God without being sent on mission to do the work of God."[52]

This, then, is the final path of spiritual formation: preparation for and engagement with mission. And the spiritual practice that best prepares us for this path is the liturgy—both the Mass and the Liturgy of the Hours. These are the antidotes to the privatized religion of modernity. When I open the Roman Missal or the books of the Hours, I do not find there the self-expression of my individual consciousness in response to a generic divine. I find the same prayers that will be prayed by all the priests of the Roman rite—whatever their language—in continuity with those who have come before us and those who will come after us. This common set of prayers shapes

51. Barron, 130–131; see Plotinus, *Enneads* 6.9.

52. Barron, *Strangest Way*, 131.

us, if we allow it, to "be of the same mind, having the same love, being in full accord and of one mind" (Phil. 2.2), as Paul enjoins us. Isn't it striking that in the wisdom of the Church priests are "*urged* to engage in mental prayer regularly" but "are *obliged* to carry out the liturgy of the hours daily according to the proper and approved liturgical books"?[53] The Church knows that it needs its priests on the same page—literally.

The personal prayer of priests in the Liturgy of the Hours is then geared toward forming them to celebrate the greater liturgy of the Holy Mass. A major part of a seminarian's spiritual formation, therefore, is his liturgical formation. When it comes to the celebration of the liturgy, Barron offers this insight: "Good liturgy is the result of a balanced play between priest, people, and rite. When the first becomes exaggerated, we find the clerical abuse of the liturgy; when the second is overstressed, we encounter the congregationalist abuse; and when the third is exaggerated, we have the ritualistic problem. These three elements are meant to go together in a kind of coherence, a kind of dance or ballet."[54]

The seminary should be like a "conservatory" in which men are trained in this "ballet." Seminarians should be exposed to the best liturgy in the seminary that the formation faculty can offer, with good music, proper rubrics, and fine homilies. Some may ask why seminaries strive to offer such a proper liturgical experience, when, for the most part, it will not be like that in the parish. Well, it's a pretty simple reason: seminary formators try to demonstrate the proper way to celebrate the liturgy so that when the seminarian is

53. Code of Canon Law 276 §2, vatican.va (emphasis added).

54. Barron with Allen Jr., *To Light a Fire*, 145–146.

ordained and sent into parish ministry, he can bring this training and experience to his parochial community.

The priest must be the one who leads the community in prayer, and he must learn to celebrate the sacred mysteries wisely and well. The result is transformative, as Barron explains: "The liturgy is a ritual acting out of the divine *ordo* revealed in the dying and rising of Jesus and, as such, it is a continual summons to transform the dysfunctional 'city of man' into the 'City of God.'"[55]

CONCLUSION

At the beginning of this section of the book, I mentioned that I saw Ignatius of Loyola's words "Go and set the world ablaze" while attending a training program for priestly formation. That program—the Institute for Priestly Formation—has a mantra that perfectly summarizes the contents of this chapter: relationship, identity, mission. They insist, as I have throughout this book, that mission flows from identity—that what we *do* must flow from who we *are*. But they also insist that relationship comes prior even to identity. In this chapter on spiritual formation, I have shown that who we *are* flows from who we *know*—the Eucharistic Lord—who gives us our life and our identity.

For Bishop Barron, Christianity is not so much about a system of beliefs or a philosophy. It is about following a person, a divine person with two natures, human and divine, Jesus Christ our Lord, who gives us to ourselves and calls us to give to others. That does not mean, however, that Barron (or Christianity itself) is anti-

55. Robert Barron, *Heaven in Stone and Glass: Experiencing the Spirituality of the Great Cathedrals* (New York: Crossroad, 2000), 118.

intellectual. Intellectual formation is extremely important for priestly formation, and that is the subject of the next chapter.

CHAPTER 6

The Intellectual Dimension

When Queen Elizabeth II died in 2022, a story related by her long-time bodyguard, Royal Protection Officer Richard Griffin, circulated in the media. It seems that the queen enjoyed venturing out of her summer residence in Scotland to a secluded area for picnics, often with Griffin as company. One day, a couple of Americans were strolling through the countryside and came upon them. The two parties began exchanging pleasantries, and when the queen explained she had a summer home in the area and had been coming there for eighty years, the American man declared, "Well if you've been coming here for eighty years, you must have seen the queen." The monarch smartly replied, "Well, I haven't, but Dick here meets with her regularly." The Americans immediately began to treat Griffin as a man of great importance, and they asked his elderly female companion (the Queen of England!) to take a picture of the two of them with this bodyguard, before Griffin offered to also take a picture of them with Elizabeth. The Americans left the scene, and Griffin and the queen could only speculate whether those tourists would go home and be showing their photo album to their friends and family when someone would shout out to them, "You're standing next to the Queen of England!"[1]

This story reminds me of John 4, when the Samaritan woman meets Jesus at the well. Jesus tells her, "If you knew the gift of God, and who it is that is saying to you, 'Give me a drink,' you would have asked him, and he would have given you living water" (John 4:10). Just as the clueless Americans were so eager to hear about the Queen of England that they failed to realize that she was talking to them, so the woman at the well is talking to the incarnate Son of God—the Word who was in the beginning with God and through whom all things were made—and all she could see was an ordinary Jewish man. Unlike the queen, however, Jesus is eager to reveal himself to her, although only in stages. She begins to see the power of God in Jesus and responds, "I see that you are a prophet" (John 4:19). By the end of the conversation, she accepts him as the Messiah and goes to tell everyone she knows about their encounter. But even then, his divinity remains hidden from her, only to be revealed after his Death, Resurrection, and Ascension into heaven.

In the last chapter, I stressed the importance of relationship with Jesus—that ideas about God are not sufficient; we need to have a real relationship with him, "a listening and learning heart," as the *Program of Priestly Formation* insists. However, the modern-day story of the clueless Americans and the biblical story of the woman at the well show that the converse is also true: to really *know* God *relationally*, we do have to *know about* him also. The Americans were in conversation with the queen, but they didn't recognize

1. Margherita Cole, "Naive U.S. Tourist Asked the Queen to Take a Photo of Him With Her Bodyguard," *My Modern Met*, September 14, 2022, https://mymodernmet.com/queen-elizabeth-ii-bodyguard-story/.

who she was, so they didn't approach her in a manner befitting her dignity. Even if they had realized that she was the queen, though, they would have had a hard time really appreciating who she was without knowing the history of the monarchy in England, her family history, the history of World War II, and so on. While the woman at the well was in conversation with Jesus and came to revere him, she did not know the story of his birth, the true scope of his mission, or ultimately his ontological dignity as the very one that she should actually be worshiping.

Our culture is full of people like the woman at the well—led by their desires into sin and shame, confused about religious principles, and unable to see in the Church (the Body of Christ) the God who wishes to save them. Robert Barron has shown that this situation requires priests who are lovers of Jesus, first and foremost, but also mystagogues and soul doctors. *The Program of Priestly Formation* states, "The basic principle of intellectual formation for priesthood candidates is noted in *Pastores Dabo Vobis*, no. 51: 'For the salvation of their brothers and sisters, they should seek an ever deeper knowledge of the divine mysteries.'"[2] If we are to be mystagogues, we must know the divine mysteries! And if we are to be soul doctors, we have to know the workings of the human soul. This requires study.

As someone who currently serves as a professor and used to serve as an academic dean (the director of intellectual formation of a seminary), I must admit that I have a particular interest in this dimension of formation of the Catholic priest. I strongly believe the *Program of Priestly Formation* when it insists that "there is a reciprocal

2. *Program of Priestly Formation* 226, 6th ed. (Washington, DC: United States Conference of Catholic Bishops, 2022).

relationship between spiritual and intellectual formation" and that "intellectual formation is integral to what it means to be human."[3] In many ways, this entire book is an homage to the role that Robert Barron has played in my own ongoing intellectual formation as a priest and his insistence that "dumbing down" the faith robs our spiritual lives and pastoral activity of real fruitfulness. Hence, in this chapter, I will begin by considering how to keep intellectual formation integrated with the other dimensions of formation. Then, I will go on to explore the relevance of St. Thomas Aquinas—Bishop Barron's primary theological muse—to this formation.

INTELLECTUAL FORMATION—FINDING THE RIGHT BALANCE

In the case of some seminarians who are more scholastically inclined, the intellectual dimension of formation to the priesthood can become predominant. I have to admit that this was the case for me many times in my years of formation, especially on the college seminary level. This desire for the academic life was so strong in me that my formator after my freshman year of college handed me the vocation information to the New York Province of the Society of Jesus (Jesuits), a religious order known for its commitment to the intellectual apostolate. My own brother, who had a Jesuit education, tried to convince me to join "God's marines," as they used to be called. I did think about it, but I came away sensing firmly the call to serve as a diocesan priest. I did not know at the time that I would end up serving primarily in seminaries, a diocesan priest in the academic world.

3. *Program of Priestly Formation* 261.

I do not think we should discourage men who are drawn primarily at first to the intellectual dimension of the priesthood by insisting too quickly for them to find the perfect balance between the human, spiritual, and pastoral aspects of formation. As I discussed in chapter 2, Robert Barron has tried to make the call to be a mystagogue and soul doctor as exciting to brilliant young men as being a lawyer or a brain surgeon. There certainly is a need for theological and philosophical professors in our seminaries and in the great religious orders like the Jesuits, Dominicans, Franciscans, Cistercians, Benedictines, and so on. But also, Barron argued, we should recognize that working in a parish setting is inherently *intellectually* exciting. Just as a surgeon is excited to put his skills to use helping people with their medical issues, a priestly soul doctor can and should become excited to put his theological knowledge to use helping people with their spiritual issues.

So, the key is not to quash youthful enthusiasm for study but to have a seminary culture that integrates the other dimensions of formation and slowly enables the "brilliant mind" to also form his heart, soul, and strength. On the other hand, the *Program of Priestly Formation* notes that many seminarians struggle at first with their studies—older vocations who "have lost contact with formal patterns of study in school," international students, or those narrowly educated in college without adequate exposure to the liberal arts.[4] It counsels that "educational standards should not be so rigid or restrictive as to close the door" to these men; rather, the seminary should help them "so that their academic deficiencies should be overcome."[5] For these men, I like to talk about examples like Blessed

4. *Program of Priestly Formation* 266.

5. *Program of Priestly Formation* 312.

Stanley Rother and St. Jean-Marie Vianney, whose early academic struggles did not keep them from surpassing their brother priests in holiness.

Too often in some seminaries, the intellectual has been the dimension of priestly formation that is emphasized above all else. Get good grades and keep the rules, and you can get ordained. This is a particular danger in seminaries where the formation faculty is also the teaching faculty. The opposite can also be true in a seminary that is a house of formation and entrusts the intellectual formation of its seminarians to a separate academic institution such as a university. Without the day in and day out interaction of seeing a seminarian in a classroom, a formation faculty can begin to base most of its evaluation of the seminarian on how he is "in house" and ignore a quarter of his progress in formation as long as he comes home with good grades. If this is the case, seminarians can come to regard their studies as simple hurdles to overcome that are easily set aside for the "real life" of pastoral work, which then becomes intellectually shallow and culturally beige. Therefore, whatever their institutional configuration, seminaries need to strive for integration.

The *Program of Priestly Formation* suggests that "the first task of intellectual formation is to acquire a personal knowledge of the Lord Jesus Christ, who is the fullness and completion of God's Revelation and the one Teacher."[6] The formation of one's intellect does not end with seminary classes but "is continuously appropriated and deepened, so that it becomes more and more part of the disciple."[7] Therefore, if I may have a word with my fellow workers in the

6. *Program of Priestly Formation* 263.

7. *Program of Priestly Formation* 263.

vineyard of seminary formation: ongoing intellectual formation is part of your own personal task as well! I think anyone would recognize that I, as an intellectual formator, need to nurture my spiritual life, but the converse is also true. Spiritual formation faculty should continue to learn dogmatic and systematic theology. Human formation faculty should spend some time on serious philosophy. Some of this can be accomplished through one's own reading and some through conversation with colleagues. I have been blessed to engage in fruitful conversation with my colleagues who work in human, spiritual, and pastoral formation, but I think we have to be vigilant in taking the time to enrich ourselves and one another in all dimensions of our priestly life. In this way, we can overcome potential imbalances and give a good example to our students.

As excited as I was to learn theology in seminary, the *Program of Priestly Formation* points out that "this knowledge is not simply for personal possession but is destined to be shared in the community of faith."[8] I won't speak for other seminary professors, but personally, what I have heard in the classroom, I want to shout from the rooftops! (see Matt. 10:27). This is why I have wanted to write newspaper columns and books. The *Program of Priestly Formation* stresses that the good intellectual formation of a seminarian leads to him becoming "adequately skilled in communicating his knowledge to as many people as possible."[9]

Moreover, "the intellectual formation program must emphasize the intrinsic relationship between the knowledge gained in theological formation and the ecclesial dimensions of priestly service."[10]

8. *Program of Priestly Formation* 263.
9. *Program of Priestly Formation* 264.
10. *Program of Priestly Formation* 265.

This notion of the ecclesial dimension of theological studies was also stressed by Cardinal Gerhard Müller, Prefect-Emeritus of the Congregation for the Doctrine of the Faith, in a talk to seminarians:

> If the ultimate concern of theology is bringing people into the living dynamic of revelation and the response of faith, then this concern must burn all the more in the hearts of priests who have been ordained for the Church and are sacramentally configured to Christ the bridegroom who laid down his life for his bride, the Church.[11]

Cardinal Müller suggests that studying should be an act of pastoral charity for the people a priest will serve. He explains that it requires *taking on the heart of Christ*, who was moved with pity for the crowds who were like sheep without a shepherd. Müller states, "As disciples of the Good Shepherd, who came to serve and to lay down his life for the sheep, priests must never lose sight of the pastoral goal of theological reflection, and that goal is no less than the salvation of souls."[12] He suggests that if this truth is not firmly established in the minds of American Catholic theologians and ministers, they can be tossed in the wind when problems arise, following whatever trend pleases either them or their audience (see Eph. 4:14).

This waffling can be a problem if the priest deviates from Catholic doctrine. The *Program of Priestly Formation* insists that "as a man of the Church, the priest preaches and teaches fidelity

11. Gerhard L. Müller, "The Wisdom of the Priest," lecture, Knights of Columbus website, April 1, 2015, http://www.kofc.org/en/columbia/detail/wisdom-of-the-priest.html (site discontinued).

12. Müller, "The Wisdom of the Priest."

to the Magisterium, particularly the Holy Father and the diocesan bishop."[13] But it can also be a problem if the priest teaches the latest theological opinion as a spiritual fact from the pulpit. Theological scholars need to speculate on the divine mysteries and work toward advances in understanding and doctrine, but the people of God don't need these fine cocktails of academic debate; they need the meat and potatoes of the Gospel, served in an appealing way. The *Program of Priestly Formation* advises, "Contemporary expressions are always to be presented with due deference to the Tradition and in continuity with it."[14]

One reason that I so often recommend the theology of Bishop Barron is that it is rooted in the long intellectual tradition of the Church. While he may sometimes be "trending" on social media, Barron is not simply trendy. He urges his readers to heed the wisdom of the saints, the Doctors of the Church, the teaching of the *Catechism*, and the riches of the Scriptures. Chief among those saints and doctors in the history of the Church is the Angelic Doctor, Thomas Aquinas, whom the *Program of Priestly Formation* calls a "model and guide" for the intellectual formation of seminarians for the priesthood.[15]

NON NISI TE DOMINE: TOMMASO D'AQUINO AND ROBERT OF CHICAGO

If you spend any time listening to Bishop Barron, it becomes apparent how widely read he is in Christian theology, history, and literature. Nevertheless, a discerning eye will clearly see that chief

13. *Program of Priestly Formation* 265.
14. *Program of Priestly Formation* 354.
15. *Program of Priestly Formation* 347.

among his theological masters stands St. Thomas Aquinas. Barron acknowledges, time and again, the supreme influence that the great medieval theologian of the Order of Preachers has had on his thought from the beginning. He recounts to John L. Allen Jr. in *To Light a Fire on the Earth*,

> It was at Fenwick High School, I'm a freshman and it's springtime, so the end of my first year. We were out at the playground, horsing around, so we all come in kind of sweating, and it's time for religion class. We had this young Dominican, Father Thomas Paulsen. That day, he laid out for us the Aquinas arguments for the existence of God, beginning, I think, with the motion argument. There I was, a fourteen-year-old Catholic kid just going to Mass, and I still don't know why, but I was captivated. I think it was a movement of grace, and I'm sure that no one else in that class was all that interested. For some reason, however, it struck me as, Wow, that's right, that's correct. No one up to that point in my experience really had thought seriously about God, you just went to Mass. . . . That exposure to Aquinas showed me you could actually think deeply and clearly about God. Not that I didn't believe in God, I did, but there was rational depth and clarity to Aquinas that hit me like a revelation.[16]

Barron went on to write his doctoral dissertation on a comparison between Thomas and the Protestant thinker Paul Tillich, who was so influential at the time. One can see the influence of Tillich

16. Robert Barron with John L. Allen Jr., *To Light a Fire on the Earth: Proclaiming the Gospel in a Secular Age* (New York: Image Books, 2017), 19.

in Barron's articles on "Priest as Bearer of the Mystery"[17] as well as in his classic book *And Now I See.*[18] Moreover, he has often spoken of how his theological education was suffused with the writings of the German theologian Karl Rahner and how his encounter with the Swiss theologian Hans Urs von Balthasar brought about a Christocentric revolution in his thinking.[19]

Nevertheless, St. Thomas—more than Balthasar, more than Tillich—is Barron's true theological muse. He says so explicitly in his first book, the magnificent *Thomas Aquinas: Spiritual Master.* When he became a bishop, he chose as his episcopal motto the phrase *Non Nisi Te Domine.* This refers to one of the most common stories told about St. Thomas. As Barron describes it,

> Toward the end of his life, after having struggled to compose a text on the Eucharist, Thomas, in an act of spiritual bravado not in keeping with his quiet nature, hurled his book at the foot of the crucifix, inviting Christ himself to pass judgment. According to the well-known account of this episode, a voice came from the statue of the crucified Jesus announcing that Thomas had written well concerning the sacrament and offering him a reward in recompense for his labors: "What would you have?" the voice asked. "*Non nisi te, Domine*" (nothing but you, Lord), responded the saint. It is my conviction that this mystical conversation between servant and Master is a sort of interpretive key to the

17. Robert Barron, "Priest as Bearer of the Mystery," *Church* (Summer 1994).

18. Robert Barron, *And Now I See: A Theology of Transformation* (Park Ridge, IL: Word on Fire Academic, [1998] 2021). Tillich's influence is especially evident in chapter 5.

19. See, for instance, Barron, "How Von Balthasar Changed My Mind," in *Renewing Our Hope: Essays for the New Evangelization* (Washington, DC: The Catholic University of America Press, 2020), 65–84.

> whole of Aquinas' life and thought: he wanted nothing more than Christ, nothing other than Christ, nothing less than Christ.[20]

As for the master, so for the disciple. "Nothing but you, Lord" is the key to understanding the theology of Robert Barron as well, particularly his theology of the priesthood that I have been discussing.

In recommending Thomas to readers today, Barron recognizes that barriers to entry exist for those who want to study Aquinas. Those who open Thomas' most famous work, the *Summa theologiae* (summation of theology), are often bewildered by the Scholastic style typical of the high Middle Ages. In the *Summa*,[21] Thomas proceeds systematically through the subject of sacred doctrine (*sacra doctrina*) with a series of questions and answers. For each question (*disputatio*), he first offers several wrong answers or objections; these are followed by a quotation from Scripture or another authority to refute the wrong answers (*sed contra*); this in turn is followed by Thomas' own response (*respondeo*); and each question concludes with a point-by-point reply to the objections. While this style can seem dry to us today, it was based on a practice common to medieval scriptural masters that was anything but. Barron explains that a master professor was required

> to raise and resolve those thorny questions that emerged from biblical commentary. The major forum for this theological exploration was the event that the medievals called a *quaestio*

20. Robert Barron, *Thomas Aquinas: Spiritual Master* (Park Ridge, IL: Word on Fire Academic, [1996] 2022), 1.

21. Thomas did write another *Summa*, the *Summa contra Gentiles*, but it's still typical to call the *Summa theologiae* (*ST*) simply "the *Summa*," as I do here.

> *disputata*, a disputed question. A disputed question took place in public, the master presiding over a large and sometimes raucous group of students and faculty. In a lively exchange, he would entertain objections from the floor, respond to the best of his ability, and finally resolve the question at hand, perhaps reveling in cheers or enduring catcalls from the floor. Thomas Aquinas was the most respected master of the *quaestio disputata* in Paris. Obviously, many professors carefully avoided this high-pressured and potentially embarrassing forum, but Thomas seemed to thrive in it, disputing far more often than any of his colleagues.[22]

The closest analogue we have today might be a Catholic radio show, in which any average person can call in and pose problems that the apologist must solve; Bishop Barron himself has sometimes hosted an internet version of this open forum, inviting atheists and other critics of the Catholic faith to pose difficult questions to him through an "Ask Me Anything" (AMA) on Reddit. Thomas' *Summa*, then, is an idealized version of a series of such Q&A sessions on the topic of the fundamentals of the faith, although offering only serious and weighty objections and leaving out the "cheers and catcalls."

It helps in understanding Thomas to picture him as an oasis of spiritual calm and determination in the midst of a roiling sea of spiritual fervor and fierce disagreement in the thirteenth century. He was born in 1225 in Roccasecca in the county of Aquino (in present-day Italy) to Landolfo, a wealthy landowner, and his wife, Theodora.[23] Thomas' biographer Jean-Pierre Torrell writes, "As the

22. Barron, *Thomas Aquinas*, 7.

23. Hence, he is Tommaso d'Aquino—Thomas from Aquino. Aquinas (the Latin form of Aquino) is not a last name in our sense, but refers to the county of Thomas' birth.

youngest son in the family, Thomas was destined, as was the custom of his era, for the Church. Given its close proximity, Monte Cassino left little room for any alternative."[24] Monte Cassino was a long-established and highly influential Benedictine abbey, founded by St. Benedict himself nearly eight hundred years earlier. Torrell adds that "Landolfo offered his son as an oblate to the monastery, probably with the ulterior motive that Thomas might someday become abbot."[25] Thomas thus left home to study there at the monastery at the age of five (talk about young vocations!). However, around high-school age (fourteen or fifteen), at the advice of the abbot, his parents sent him to the bustling city of Naples for further study.

Just as Robert Barron had been enthralled at age fourteen by encountering the thought of Aquinas, the young Thomas had his mind and heart set ablaze by encounters with a radical new religious order founded by Dominic Guzman, called the Order of Preachers or Dominicans. Like the Franciscans, the Dominicans were mendicants who did not stay in a stable monastery but went out among the people preaching and begging for their sustenance. Without consulting his parents, young Thomas took the Dominican habit in Naples. So enraged were Landolfo and Theodora that their son wanted to run off and join this new, radical form of religious life that they imprisoned him at home! Although they tried various means to dissuade him—famously including a prostitute[26]—in the end, Thomas prevailed. He left for Paris to study under the

24. Jean-Pierre Torrell, *Thomas Aquinas: His Life and Work*, 3rd ed. (Washington, DC: The Catholic University of America Press, 2023), 6. This is the latest edition of the biography that Barron relies upon in *Thomas Aquinas: Spiritual Master*.

25. Torrell, 6. Some say that Thomas had an uncle who had been abbot of the monastery, but Torrell makes no mention of such a figure.

26. Torrell mentions this incident only in passing but doesn't seem to question it (12).

Dominican friar and teacher St. Albert the Great (1200–1280), and he was destined to become a master of sacred theology himself.

In order to understand St. Thomas, it is essential for us to grasp that his primary responsibility was to comment on Sacred Scripture. While he had a profound appreciation of philosophy, especially Aristotle,[27] in works like the *Summa theologiae* he is expounding *sacra doctrina*—the sacred doctrine contained in Scripture, handed down by Tradition, clarified by the Magisterium of the Church, and ultimately given for the salvation of mankind. Barron comments, "As he says in the very first article of the *Summa theologiae*, the entire purpose of theology is to raise believers outside of and beyond themselves to a union with the God who cannot fully be grasped. . . . His thought is meant to be above all a guide, a series of landmarks on the journey into God."[28]

For Thomas, theology is all about the "systematic unpacking of the divinely revealed truth" of God.[29] This leads him to write in a very orderly, even impersonal style that turns some readers off. Worse, some learned critics have suggested that Thomas "'thinks' his way to God, basing his entire theology on rational proofs and philosophical arguments. There seems to be, some say, a sort of hubris or dangerous pride in this approach, a certain lack of docility and humility before the mystery of God."[30] Barron responds that this impression mistakes style for substance. Thomas is the same friar

27. And he continues to have a profound impact on philosophers. See, for instance, Pasquale Porro, *Thomas Aquinas: A Historical and Philosophical Profile*, trans. Joseph G. Trabbic and Roger W. Nutt (Washington, DC: The Catholic University of America Press, 2017).

28. Barron, *Thomas Aquinas*, 3.

29. See John P. Cush, *The How-To Book of Catholic Theology: Everything You Need to Know but No One Ever Taught You* (Huntington, IN: Our Sunday Visitor, 2020).

30. Barron, *Thomas Aquinas*, 15.

who wrote profound Eucharist hymns, such as "Adoro Te Devote," that still fuel Catholic devotion today. Barron insists, "When one interprets Thomas merely as a rationalist philosopher or theologian, one misses the burning heart of everything he wrote. Aquinas was a saint deeply in love with Jesus Christ, and the image of Christ pervades the entire edifice that is his philosophical, theological and scriptural work."[31]

He explains that, according to Thomas, we human beings are created to lose ourselves, following the example of Jesus Christ, who as God and man is himself "the coming together of two Ecstasies."[32] Poetically, Barron elaborates, "Jesus reveals the ecstasy that is God in the measure that he, as a human being, is ecstasy before God. Jesus becomes transparent to God's self-forgetting because he, in his humanity, is nothing but self-forgetting love. In a word, the person of Jesus Christ is the joining of two ecstasies, the moment when the passionate human thirst for God meets the equally passionate divine thirst for us."[33]

Like Robert Barron himself, Thomas Aquinas loved the Lord Jesus passionately, and as a member of the Order of Preachers, Thomas had a thirst to communicate that love—a love that cannot be hidden, a love that cannot be denied—to "as many people as possible."[34] Barron offers an alternative way to think about Thomas' theological style:

31. Barron, 1.

32. See Barron, "Jesus Christ: The Coming Together of Two Ecstasies," in *Thomas Aquinas*, 15–36.

33. Barron, *Thomas Aquinas*, 29.

34. *Program of Priestly Formation* 264.

> Why are there so many questions, so many articles, so many objections and responses in the *Summa*? One might respond: because there are so many ways that the sinful soul can evade the call to Christlike obedience and openness of heart. Like Ignatius and John of the Cross, Thomas is extremely sensitive to the darkness of the spirit, to the labyrinthine ways of sin, and, again like those two great masters of the soul, he has the patience and the love required to seek out the sinner despite all obstacles. Thomas will not rest until his reader is lured into wonder and ecstasy.[35]

THE ANGELIC DOCTOR AS AN INTELLECTUAL MODEL

Understanding what Thomas wrote is no easy task. Speaking personally, I must admit that I wish I knew him better. Given that I've been called to the intellectual formation of future priests, this deficit is one of the biggest regrets in my life, and if I had another allotted time for study in the course of my priestly ministry, I would devote it exclusively to the study of the *Doctor Communis*.[36] My own theological training, for which I am very grateful, focused more on Sacred Scripture and Sacred Tradition, as well as theologians of the *Nouvelle théologie*[37] like Hans Urs von Balthasar, Yves Congar,

35. Barron, *Thomas Aquinas*, 36.

36. This is Latin for the "Common Doctor," a term applied to St. Thomas because his thought can be universally applied in theology. He is also known as *Doctor Angelicus* ("Angelic Doctor") due to his holiness of life and his writings on the angels of God.

37. The *Nouvelle théologie* is part of the *ressourcement* (literally, "return to the sources," from the French) movement that began in the 1920s and had a major impact on the theology of the Second Vatican Council.

Henri de Lubac,[38] and Joseph Ratzinger (Pope Benedict XVI),[39] and not as much on actually reading St. Thomas. When I was in the college-level seminary studying philosophy, we read more about what Jesuit Fathers Frederick Copleston[40] and Bernard Lonergan[41] (and other commentators) said about Thomas than what Thomas actually wrote!

I appreciate the Angelic Doctor more and more for his clarity and see the absolute necessity of his theological framework. While I still recognize the role that the positive theology in which I was trained must play, I think we need to be enriched by what Scholastic theology at its best has to offer.[42] We are seeing more and more that Aquinas is someone who builds his thought on the Bible. Thomas is also one of the clearest synthesizers of the Fathers of the Church. Indeed, he cites St. Augustine almost more than he cites any other source.[43] For those looking for contextual theology—that

38. Henri de Lubac (1896–1891) was a French Jesuit and an important theologian of the twentieth century. He was created a cardinal by Pope St. John Paul II in 1983. Bishop Barron speaks of the necessity of a "de Lubac Option" for Catholicism in the twenty-first century. See "Bishop Barron on Cardinal Etchegaray, Henri de Lubac, and Vatican II," Aleteia, September 20, 2019, https://aleteia.org/2019/09/20/bishop-barron-on-cardinal-etchegaray-henri-de-lubac-and-vatican-ii/.

39. Joseph Ratzinger (1927–2022) became Pope Benedict XVI.

40. Frederick Copleston (1907–1994) was an English Jesuit priest who produced a multivolume history of philosophy that is still one of the finest works available on the subject in the English language.

41. Bernard Lonergan (1904–1984) was a Canadian theologian and philosopher. And the subject of my dissertation! Bishop Barron writes on the importance of Lonergan in "Why Bernard Lonergan Matters for Pastoral People," in *Exploring Catholic Theology: Essays on God, Liturgy, and Evangelization* (Grand Rapids, MI: Baker Academic, 2015) as well as in "The Fetishism of Dialogue," Word on Fire, May 20, 2009, https://www.wordonfire.org/resources/article/the-fetishism-of-dialogue/347/.

42. See Cush, *The How-To Book of Catholic Theology*, for an explanation of the terms "positive theology" and "Scholastic theology."

43. Aquinas is, at his essence—even more than a gifted philosopher—a brilliant commentator not only on Sacred Scripture but also Sacred Tradition. Stephen Beale, in his

is, looking for a theology that embraces other cultures and other disciplines—St. Thomas Aquinas' use of the philosophies of the Muslim philosopher Averroes and the pagan philosopher Aristotle offer a true model of critical inculturation.

Therefore, I recommend the study of Thomas himself, with Robert Barron's *Thomas Aquinas: Spiritual Master* and other writings as an orientation. There are many more splendid books of introduction to the Angelic Doctor.[44] There's now even an *Aquinas 101* video series on YouTube put up by the Thomistic Institute, a dynamic group of Dominicans on the American east coast. But for the remainder of this chapter, I want to discuss four ways that Thomas is also a model to imitate for the intellectual formation of seminarians for the priesthood.[45]

incredible article in the *National Catholic Register* "Which Church Fathers Most Influenced St. Thomas Aquinas?" (January 28, 2020, https://www.ncregister.com/blog/which-church-fathers-most-influenced-st-thomas-aquinas), breaks it all down for us clearly: St. Augustine of Hippo is quoted by St. Thomas in the *Summa theologiae* 3,156 times! Here's the rest of Mr. Beale's analysis regarding how often St. Thomas quotes various Church Fathers:

1) Gregory the Great: 761 times
2) Dionysius: 607
3) Jerome: 377
4) John Damascene: 367
5) John Chrysostom: 309
6) Ambrose: 284
7) Isidore: 162
8) Origen: 84
9) Basil: 56
10) Gregory of Nyssa: 53
11) Athanasius: 45
12) Cyril: 28

44. See especially Jean-Pierre Torrell's masterful two-volume work on Thomas Aquinas: *Saint Thomas Aquinas*, vol. 1, *The Person and His Work*, rev. ed., trans. Robert Royal (Washington, DC: The Catholic University of America Press, 2005); *Saint Thomas Aquinas*, vol. 2, *Spiritual Master*, trans. Robert Royal (Washington, DC: The Catholic University of America Press, 2003).

45. *Program of Priestly Formation* 347.

Arguing for the Faith in Good Faith

While I've never seen a theologian today—even a Thomist—write in quite the style of the *Summa*, Thomas' work is nevertheless a great model of intellectual clarity and charity. It is not only that Thomas incorporated the insights of everyone he read, especially non-Catholic philosophers like Aristotle and Averroes. The way in which St. Thomas wrote the *Summa* also shows that he has already considered all of the most relevant and potent objections that one could make to his arguments. Indeed, it's often said that Thomas formulates the arguments of his opponents better than they did!

This clarity and charity is part of the secret to the evangelical success of Robert Barron as well. He is always willing to grant whatever is true in his opponents' arguments and to acknowledge the force of their objections, even when he's convinced that they are wrong in their final conclusions. For example, one can find on YouTube a video of a talk by Barron (at the University of St. Thomas in Minnesota) titled "Aquinas and Why the New Atheists Are Right." Of course, Barron does not mean the new atheists are right to deny God; rather, he suggests that they are right to reject the image of God that they have gotten from bad preaching and bad theology. A truly metaphysical approach to God, such as is found in Aquinas, overcomes these objections not by denying their force but by better understanding who and what God is and is not.[46]

I think this intellectual fearlessness is so important to becoming mystagogues and soul doctors in today's Church. There are a plethora of reasons that people doubt the faith or resist the invitation to grace, and many of them are quite profound—with (apparent) scientific

46. See the section below on the noncompetitiveness of God.

backing at times. If we are dismissive or respond with pat answers and straw man arguments, we make it seem that the faith is weak intellectual sauce, unable to really cope with the modern world. On the contrary, we should go out of our way to acknowledge whatever is true, good, or beautiful in the arguments against some aspect of the faith, without agreeing with their conclusions that lead to dissent, heresy, or apostasy. If we do not have the talents of a Thomas to defeat rival philosophies in intellectual combat, I nevertheless believe that by the grace of the Holy Spirit—and if we take the time to study—we can probably at least offer some insight to those we encounter with questions, perhaps a different way of looking at a problem than that person had considered. This may give the person something to ponder and may plant a seed for a later conversation or even conversion. It may also mean that we learn something new ourselves! But for either of these things to happen, we have to listen attentively and with respect, as Thomas did, to *sacra doctrina* and the voice of the Lord.

Showing People that They Need God

It can be a temptation to think that theology is just a highly specialized subject for a select few that is of little concern to average people with their "real-life" problems. Nothing could be further from the truth! In the very first question of the *Summa theologiae*, St. Thomas concludes, "It is therefore necessary that besides philosophical science there should be a sacred science learned through revelation." Thomas does not simply accept and expound *sacra doctrina*—he argues that it's a "must have." So, too, in our time, we as priests must be prepared and eager to give reasons to our people as to why following and learning about God is not just a lifestyle choice but a necessity.

Barron comments, "What exactly is theology . . . and why is it necessary? . . . We require a science beyond the philosophical and natural sciences precisely because we human beings are oriented to an end that surpasses our powers of rational comprehension. We are destined to be united to a power that is beyond whatever the eye can see or the mind can know, beyond the world in all of its richness, beyond the web of contingent things."[47]

At the heart of every human life is a great question—how can I be happy? Nothing could be more relevant to real life than this. At the beginning of the *Prima Secundae*—the first half of the second part of the *Summa*—Thomas shows how all of the ways in which people seek happiness go astray.[48] Barron explains, "Any attempt to root our lives in something other than God—in ego, money, power, praise, pleasure—will set up an unbearable tension, a sort of crisis of the heart."[49] As priests, we need to take up this invitation of the Angelic Doctor to show our people how their lesser goods will never satisfy, but that Christ alone will satisfy. We need not present the faith simply as a set of things to be believed or obligations but as an answer to this great human desire for happiness, this longing for the true Good that does not fade or falter. Barron elaborates, "All individual acts of the will rest upon, depend upon, the final and all-embracing desire for the good itself—which is none other than God. . . . To be fully itself, the will must give itself radically to this good. . . . The will finds itself in surrendering to the good that is its ground and end and *raison d'être*."[50]

47. Barron, *Thomas Aquinas*, 17.

48. This so-called "Treatise on Happiness" is *Summa theologiae* 1-2.1–5. See https://www.newadvent.org/summa/2.htm.

49. Barron, *Thomas Aquinas*, 12.

50. Barron, 33–34.

Insist on God as Mystery

Both in answering objections and stirring up people's desire for true happiness, Barron often points back to the classical doctrine of God's transcendence as received and enriched by Thomas Aquinas. If we are to be mystagogues, we have to remember and communicate that God—the one God in three persons—is a great mystery! This does not mean that we can say nothing at all meaningful about the Trinity (as too many priests seem to do on Trinity Sunday), because that would mean that the incredible revelation of God's inner life means nothing for our lives. But it does mean that we have to clear away the idea that God the Father is a basically more powerful and exalted version of one of us creatures—perhaps a white-haired grandfather with a booming voice (and no sense of humor) hanging out in the clouds. In searching for a truer understanding of God, Thomas uses what is known as the *via negativa* in describing who and what God is.[51] Barron explains,

> Aquinas never tells us what God is, only what God is not. His entire approach is to undermine all of our idolatrous attempts to turn God into something understandable or controllable, something we could manipulate or avoid. No, he tells us in a variety of ways, the God who appears in Jesus Christ is a power that is consummately surprising, captivating, alluring. All of this strangeness is caught in Thomas' curious description of God as "simple." As we shall see in a later chapter, this means that God is not a being like other beings in the world, that God is not

51. The *via negativa*, or "negative way," often called apophatic theology, tries to come to a deeper understanding of God by stating what he is not in order to come to an understanding of what he is.

> even the highest or supreme being; God is rather Being itself, ungraspable, unknowable power.[52]

God is utterly transcendent; he is not another force acting within the world, however powerful, but the Mystery that underlies all of the universe. This metaphysical insistence is, for example, the key to understanding creation *ex nihilo* (out of nothing) and answering many modern objections to faith arising from scientific developments. But there is more.

Barron argues that when we lose this sense of God's transcendence—when we try to lump God into the same metaphysical category of "being" as his creatures—we end with a God who seems to be a rival to our freedom and fulfillment.[53] This leads to either pantheism (William James) or atheism (Jean-Paul Sartre) out of the valid concern of preserving the dignity of human freedom. As one Russian revolutionary put it, "If God is, man is a slave; now, man can and must be free; then, God does not exist."[54] Barron, through the arguments of St. Thomas, argues that this would be true if God were another being among beings like us—but he isn't. Instead, only because God is God and makes us in his image does our freedom from the world of nature make any sense!

How many of our people are leaving the faith because they are convinced that God and the Church unnecessarily impinge on their freedom and thwart their happiness! We need to have the intellectual

52. Barron, *Thomas Aquinas*, 11.

53. Robert Barron, *The Priority of Christ: Toward a Postliberal Catholicism* (Grand Rapids, MI: Baker Academic, 2007), 195. There he is discussing the conclusions of William James, who saw an active, personal God in this negative light.

54. Mikhail Bakunin, *God and the State*, trans. Benjamin Tucker (New York: Mother Earth, 1916), 25, quoted in Barron, *Renewing Our Hope*, 258.

tools to diagnose and treat these spiritually fatal conditions. The goal of theology is not, ultimately, to get them to think about these concepts as an intellectual puzzle but to use these arguments to clear away obstacles and make straight the way to encountering the living God who can show them what true freedom and happiness are. Barron writes, "Our faith is infinitely strengthened by contact with the sheer power of God's own mind; our hope is superabundantly enlivened by the conviction that God loves us so intensely that he gives us his only Son; our love is supremely awakened in response to God's overwhelming gesture of love; and, perhaps most importantly for the purposes of this book, our participation in the life of God, which is our proper end, is infinitely intensified through contact with the divinized humanity of Jesus Christ."[55]

Look to Christ as the Center

It is sometimes said that Aquinas is insufficiently Christocentric because he saves the discussion of Jesus and his life for the third part of the *Summa*. But just as the real climax happens in the third act of a drama, so in the coming of Christ, Thomas' interrogation into the nature of God and humanity reaches its zenith. The mysteries of God's transcendence and noncompetitiveness are nowhere more profoundly evident than in the Incarnation. God is so far beyond us that he can become one of us without losing his transcendence. Barron explains, "The central affirmation of classical Christianity is that in Jesus of Nazareth God and humanity met in a noncompetitive and nonviolent way."[56] We see this in the Christmas story,

55. Barron, *Thomas Aquinas*, 27.

56. Barron, *The Priority of Christ*, 17.

when Jesus comes to earth in a quiet place in Nazareth, born to a poor family in humble circumstances. But we also see it throughout Christ's life, and especially his Passion, Death, and Resurrection. Barron observes, "The crucified Jesus returned alive to those who had abused, abandoned, denied, and fled from him, but he confronted them not with threats and vengeance but with the nonviolence of compassion and forgiveness."[57]

Barron continues that "Christians concluded" from this "luminous revelation" not only that Jesus was God, but that "God's own being" is inherently "nonviolent and relational," not overpowering and domineering.[58]

Hence, there is no contradiction between speculating on the mysteries of God and contemplating the life of Jesus. There is no contradiction between classical metaphysics and Paul's declaration "I decided to know nothing among you except Jesus Christ, and him crucified" (1 Cor. 2:2). Barron, that great champion of Thomas' metaphysics of God and creation, proposes that "Christians know and seek knowledge in a distinctive way, precisely because they take the narratives concerning Jesus Christ as epistemically basic."[59] At the same time, the example of Christ—nonviolence and forgiveness—has to govern the manner in which we share this knowledge with one another and the world. Precisely because God is so mysterious and counterintuitive, precisely because he does not interfere with our freedom, we have to give people the space and time to consider our arguments and proposals and to experience God's invitation in their own lives to enter into this saving truth.

57. Barron, 17.
58. Barron, 17.
59. Barron, 19.

CONCLUSION: EVERY PRIEST A THEOLOGIAN

In conclusion, let me recall Bishop Barron's notion of the priest as soul doctor. The priest must be a professional and know his material like a medical doctor knows his material. If a doctor is not professional, people get sick and die. At the supernatural level, if we as priests don't know our material, people's souls get sick, and they die spiritually. The late Fr. Matthew Lamb argued that, like doctors, theologians should be subject to claims of malpractice![60] Priests and seminarians have a tremendous obligation, then, to study. And with St. Thomas Aquinas and Bishop Barron as models of priests passionately in love with study for the sake of holiness and pastoral service, we can learn to love the wisdom that can only come from God and learn to communicate it to a world that needs it so much.

For this reason, I contend that every priest, and the diocesan priest in particular, must be a theologian, even if he is not the specialized kind of theologian who performs research, teaches in a seminary, or serves as a censor or theological consultant. In this, I am following the late Jesuit John Courtney Murray, who writes that "the simple priest is under the necessity of being trained as a theologian because of his association in the magisterial office of the bishop."[61] We all want to be simple priests, and indeed, this should be our goal; however, we are never to be simpletons. The priest who has not kept up his reading since the day he left the seminary, who simply feeds his people with "feel-good" popcorn theology that has no basis in the intellectual tradition of the Church and the

60. Matthew Lamb, "Theological Malpractice," *National Review Online*, October 3, 2002. Reprinted in several diocesan newspapers, including *The Boston Pilot*, October 18, 2002, 13.

61. John Courtney Murray, "Toward a Theology for the Layman: The Problem of Its Finality," *Theological Studies* 5 (March 1944): 43–75, at 43.

transcendence of Almighty God, will not know how to give his people life-giving medicine and spiritual care. Murray adds, "Theology must exist in the Church; it must also exist for the Church, to serve her needs—fundamentally her need to teach the word of God."[62] In his intellectual formation, the future priest must come to know what the Church teaches, believe what the Church teaches, and communicate what the Church teaches in every situation, never changing the truth of the teaching, but striving to meet the people of God where they are and bring them to where they should be.

That is to say, good theology leads to good pastoral ministry, which is the subject of the final chapter of this book. But I want to conclude this chapter with the observation that the priest as theologian should be—in a phrase coined by Balthasar but that certainly describes St. Thomas—one who practices "kneeling theology." Even if we are not the academic types, we need not be afraid of the faithless academics who attack God or try to tear down the Church's teaching to suit modern errors.

Barron reminds us that we "will theologize more accurately about Christianity when [our] minds are formed in the concrete (and very bodily) discipline of prayer and worship."[63] One particular prayer that may be helpful is Thomas Aquinas' own prayer before study:

> Ineffable Creator, Who, from the treasures of your wisdom,
> have established three hierarchies of angels,

62. Murray, 43.

63. Robert Barron, *The Strangest Way: Walking the Christian Path* (Park Ridge, IL: Word on Fire Institute, 2021), 19–20; see Jakob Laubach, "Hans Urs von Balthasar," in *Theologians of Our Time*, ed. Leonhard Reinisch (Notre Dame, IN: University of Notre Dame Press, 1964), 146–147.

have arrayed them in marvelous order
above the fiery heavens,
and have marshaled the regions
of the universe with such artful skill,

You are proclaimed
the true font of light and wisdom,
and the primal origin
raised high beyond all things.

Pour forth a ray of your brightness
into the darkened places of my mind;
disperse from my soul
the twofold darkness
into which I was born:
sin and ignorance.

You make eloquent the tongues of infants.
refine my speech
and pour forth upon my lips
The goodness of your blessing.

Grant to me
keenness of mind,
capacity to remember,
skill in learning,
subtlety to interpret,
and eloquence in speech.

May you
guide the beginning of my work,
direct its progress,
and bring it to completion.

You who are true God and true Man,
who live and reign, world without end.

Amen.

CHAPTER 7

The Pastoral Dimension

Let's return for a moment to the story from the last chapter of the Americans who met the Queen of England and did not recognize her. This story also reminds me of Genesis 18, in which Abraham shows great hospitality to three men crossing through the desert, and they turn out to be heavenly guests who promise him that he will have a son. Abraham's generosity is the likely background for the passage from Hebrews 13:2: "Do not neglect to show hospitality to strangers, for by doing that some have entertained angels without knowing it." Imagine if those Americans had come across the queen not in the calm enjoyment of a picnic but in some kind of need or distress. How they reacted to what seemed to them like an ordinary, nice old woman could have ended up as headline news all across the world! We read in Matthew 25 that Jesus considers the hungry, the thirsty, the naked, the sick, and those in prison to be so mysteriously united to himself that how we treat them determines our final judgment: "As you did it to one of the least of these who are members of my family, you did it to me" (Matt. 25:40). This verse was fundamental to the ministry of Mother Teresa, who is famous for speaking of Jesus in the "distressing disguise of the poor."

As priests, as visible representatives of Christ on earth, our primary ministry is not the alleviation of material poverty, but rather, as I have been discussing throughout the book, to serve as mystagogues and soul doctors through Christ's three offices of priest, prophet, and king. Nevertheless, we must still exercise what the Church calls "the preferential option for the poor." The *Program of Priestly Formation* insists, "If seminarians are to be formed after the model of Jesus, the Good Shepherd, who came 'to bring glad tidings to the poor,' then they must have sustained contact with those who are privileged in God's eyes—the poor, the marginalized, the sick, and the suffering," as well as "the elderly, the disabled, those who live in isolation (such as migrants), and prisoners."[1] Rather than treating these groups as a nuisance to our preferred ministry, we have to treat them with the care that we would treat Jesus himself. Our own salvation depends upon it!

There is no contradiction, as is sometimes thought, between service to the poor and a deep Christocentric formation. It is the radical closeness of the Son of God through the Incarnation that makes supremely reasonable the upending of our usual social categories: "For, by his Incarnation, he, the son of God, *in a certain way united himself with each man*," writes John Paul II in his first encyclical, *Redemptor Hominis*.[2] The unique configuration of the priest to the person of Christ through Holy Orders also calls for a sharing in Christ's "compassion" for those who are "like sheep without a shepherd" (Matt. 9:36). The very name of the final and culminating dimension of priestly formation—pastoral—comes from the image

1. *Program of Priestly Formation* 370, 6th ed. (Washington, DC: United States Conference of Catholic Bishops, 2022).

2. John Paul II, *Redemptor Hominis* 8, encyclical letter, March 4, 1979, vatican.va.

of Christ as Good Shepherd. The *Program of Priestly Formation* says, "The basic principle of pastoral formation is enunciated in *Pastores Dabo Vobis*: 'The whole training of [seminarians] should have as its object to make them true shepherds of souls after the example of our Lord Jesus Christ, teacher, priest, and shepherd.'"[3]

As I've discussed, my primary role in seminary formation is intellectual formation, and on pastoral matters I defer to those with broader and deeper pastoral experience, who can say how practically to act as soul doctor in what Pope Francis calls the "field hospital" of the Church's front-line ministry. Robert Barron, reflecting on this image of the Holy Father, observes, "No doctor doing triage on a battlefield is going to be fussing about his patients' cholesterol or blood sugar levels. He is going to be treating major wounds and trying desperately to stop the bleeding."[4] Nor is such a doctor going to want some teaching doctor second-guessing his decisions from the safety of a med-school classroom! Nevertheless, just as teaching doctors do their best to prepare their students for what they will face on the front lines of medicine, so as a seminary formator I try to observe the Church's instruction that every aspect of priestly formation, including intellectual formation, "must be permeated by a pastoral spirit."[5]

The goal of this final chapter is to provide some insights from Robert Barron and my own experience for pastoral ministry. When I was a faculty member of the Pontifical North American College (NAC), I was blessed to give some formation talks to the seminarians.

3. *Program of Priestly Formation* 369.

4. Robert Barron, *Vibrant Paradoxes: The Both/And of Catholicism* (Park Ridge, IL: Word on Fire, 2016), 26.

5. *Ratio Fundamentalis* 119, quoted in *Program of Priestly Formation* 366.

For seminarians who are in their third year of formation, I was asked to offer some thoughts on campus ministry, since I was involved in ministry involving high school and college students before and after my ordination. When I was a seminarian at the NAC myself, the director of apostolic formation had assigned me to assist in campus ministry for the semester-abroad program for Saint Mary's College, Indiana, one of many American colleges and universities who maintain a Rome program. Later, as a very young priest, even before my bishop assigned me to teach at the high school full-time, I used to help out with the sacramental needs in some high schools in my archdiocese. My initial plans for these talks were to regale the seminarians with some of my experiences, as well as a practical list of "things-to-do and not-to-do" for a campus ministry setting. However, as I read the conference over, I realized that I did not, ultimately, have a substantial theological underpinning for the topic. To offer this theological grounding, I turned to the writings of Bishop Barron.

I began the conference by offering the seminarians the same two images of the priesthood derived from Bishop Barron that I have discussed at length in previous chapters: mystagogue and doctor of the soul. I believe that these two images of priesthood are exceptionally suited to the priest involved in campus ministry. While every student is different, many of them approach the ministry with a shocking degree of ignorance of their faith (needing a mystagogue) and of woundedness (needing a soul doctor) stemming from their family backgrounds, experiences in school, and a confusing and inhospitable culture. While most of them attending college come from relative privilege and wealth, from a spiritual and emotional perspective, I do believe they count among the poor and marginalized in this period of their lives.

In this chapter, based on my talks to those seminarians on campus ministry, I am going to follow Robert Barron's suggestion that we structure pastoral ministry around the transcendentals: the beautiful, the good, and the true, and in that particular order. The suggestions I offer in this chapter are tailored to campus ministry and, more generally, ministry among the college-educated, which is where I have the most experience and expertise. I do believe Barron's insight about the transcendental structure of evangelization in our present culture applies more generally, but I want to acknowledge that presenting the beautiful, good, and true to different populations may require other insight and ingenuity than I can offer here.

THE TRANSCENDENTALS AND THE PRIORITY OF BEAUTY

Many of the seminarians were already engaged in campus ministry in their apostolic assignments, as I had been when I was in their shoes. For some of them, it was a truly life-giving experience, and, for others, sadly, it could prove to be more of a frustration and disappointment, holding events that two or three people attended, or Masses with only a handful of congregants. The basic key, I mentioned to these young men, is not to give up. Keep being present to the students. Be there with them at meals; be where they are. Learn to take social cues when they don't want to be bothered or be involved, but take care to be with them. If few students are present, take this as a marvelous opportunity to focus on each person individually and become—as the *Program of Priestly Formation* advises—"not self-centered, aloof, judgmental, or self-imposing but instead . . . characterized by a 'serene openness' and capable of listening and collaboration."[6]

This openness is especially important in working with young people in a campus ministry setting! Within a more established setting, such as a parish or Catholic school, the priest can take a certain amount of participation for granted and therefore not work as hard on his own attitude and demeanor. But campus ministry is like any voluntary collegiate organization—if the experience is not positive for students, they will quickly scatter.

The campus minister will find that these students come to the group for many reasons. For some, it is for companionship; for others, it is for guidance; for still others, it is a chance for service, to go out and make a difference in the world; and for still others, it is a desire for the sacraments. However, if a campus minister listens attentively to the students, I believe that he will find at the core of their energy and their anxiety the same basic desires that make up every human heart: desires for truth, beauty, goodness, and unity. He must help them to understand that their deepest longings will never be satisfied by the intellectual knowledge, achievement, career, romance, or community that they seek.

Many young people today have set aside even those lesser hopes due to cynicism, painful experiences, and disappointments. The priest working in campus ministry may first have to encourage them to take their studies, their relationships, and their own lives seriously. At the same time, he must propose to them the true answer to these desires: the Mystery that we call God. The *Catechism of the Catholic Church* explains,

6. *Program of Priestly Formation* 367.

> Since our knowledge of God is limited, our language about him is equally so. We can name God only by taking creatures as our starting point, and in accordance with our limited human ways of knowing and thinking. All creatures bear a certain resemblance to God, most especially man, created in the image and likeness of God. The manifold perfections of creatures—their truth, their goodness, their beauty all reflect the infinite perfection of God. Consequently, we can name God by taking his creatures' perfections as our starting point, "for from the greatness and beauty of created things comes a corresponding perception of their Creator."[7]

These "perfections" are often called the transcendentals, and Barron suggests that they are the key to a new evangelization. John L. Allen Jr., in his interview book with Bishop Barron, gives a good summary of what Barron means by the transcendentals: "In Christian tradition, beauty, goodness, and truth are known as 'transcendentals,' linked to the three core human abilities to feel, to wish, and to think. Jesus refers to them in the Great Commandment when he talks about the mind, the soul and the heart, and inducements to take the wrong path with each of the transcendentals formed the core of his temptation scene in the Gospels."[8]

But the knowledge that the students have these fundamental desires (whether they realize it or not!) doesn't suggest a practical program for how to carry out campus ministry. However, I fully agree with Bishop Barron that we should proceed with a particular

7. *Catechism of the Catholic Church* 40–41.

8. Robert Barron with John L. Allen Jr., *To Light a Fire on the Earth: Proclaiming the Gospel in a Secular Age* (New York: Image Books, 2017), 41.

sequence in mind: we should begin by appealing to their sense of beauty, then go on to goodness, and only then focus on truth. Allen writes, "While Barron is convinced that Catholic Christianity represents the fullness of all three, he's equally convinced that the right way to open up the Catholic world to someone is with beauty," the *via pulchritudinis*.[9]

As Barron was a longtime seminary professor—as I am myself—you might think that he would want to begin with intellectual formation, especially since the students we encounter have so little of it. Why not begin with *veritas* (truth)? Bishop Barron responds,

> There's something more winsome and less threatening about the beautiful. "Just look," the evangelist might say, "at Chartres Cathedral or the Sainte Chapelle, or the Sistine Chapel ceiling, or the mosaics at Ravenna." "Just read," he might urge, "Dante's *Divine Comedy* or one of Gerard Manley Hopkins's poems, or Chesterton's *Orthodoxy*." "Just watch," he might suggest, "Mother Teresa's Missionaries of Charity at work among the poorest of the poor." The wager is that the encounter with the beautiful will naturally lead someone to ask, "What made such a thing possible?" At that point, the canny evangelizer will begin to speak of the moral behaviors and intellectual convictions that find expression in the beautiful. If I might suggest a simple metaphor, when teaching a young person the game of baseball, a good coach begins, not with the rules or with tiresome drills, but rather with the beauty of the game, with its sounds and smells and the graceful movements of its star players.[10]

9. Barron with Allen Jr., 41.
10. Barron with Allen Jr., 41.

Beginning with beauty simply makes sense; it attracts. Recall the old adage "You attract more flies with honey than vinegar." Although we may think it's necessary to increase the Christian commitment of the students by logical arguments, Joseph Ratzinger (later Pope Benedict XVI) suggested that beauty is simply a better argument:

> The only really effective apologia for Christianity comes down to two arguments, namely, the saints the Church has produced and the art which has grown in her womb. Better witness is borne to the Lord by the splendor of holiness and art which have arisen in the community of believers than by the clever excuses which apologetics has come up with to justify the dark sides which, sadly, are so frequent in the Church's human history.[11]

Above all else, the beautiful reflects and radiates the beauty of the All-Beautiful One.

Showing the treasures of the Catholic tradition to the students can be the best way to draw them into a greater discipleship that will come to fully embrace goodness and truth as well. What does this mean practically? I think that it means that early in the semester or in your relationship with the students in the ministry, you should propose opportunities to encounter beauty as your main activities. For the seminarians ministering in the Eternal City, there are an embarrassment of riches. Take the students on a tour to St. Peter's Basilica in the Vatican. Trek up to Assisi and spend time in a medieval city dedicated to the *Poverino* or to Siena to pray with Catherine.

11. Joseph Ratzinger with Vittorio Messori, *The Ratzinger Report: An Exclusive Interview on the State of the Church*, trans. Salvator Attanasio and Graham Harrison (San Francisco: Ignatius, 1985), 129.

Take the students on a "Caravaggio Run," bringing them to all the different places where the artist's works are featured. And so on.

The same is true where I am now, so near New York City. But the way of beauty is possible on any campus (or in any parish). More rural settings, while not offering as many opportunities for fine art, allow for more easily spending time as a group with the beauty of God's creation. And in any case, the media that I have found works best with students is entirely portable: good film and television. There are great films with explicitly Catholic context—such as *The Mission*, *Romero*, or *Into Great Silence*—but there is no need to limit it to those. For instance, I have used M. Night Shyamalan's *Signs* to discuss the importance of the sacraments, especially Holy Baptism, and the basic morality tales found in Rod Serling's *The Twilight Zone*. The key is not only to watch a film but to discuss it, to explain why you chose this film. For example, students may not expect a Catholic campus ministry to host a showing of Clint Eastwood's R-rated *Gran Torino*. However, it could work if you framed it by sharing a few salient points from Bishop Barron's essay on the protagonist Walt as a Christ figure.[12] Such an event would not only be thought-provoking; it would show the students that following Christ does not require hiding in a pious bunker from the harsh realities of life (such as the racist, profane characters in the film). The goal is to help teach them to use art to view the whole of reality—including sin—with a new kind of gaze given by Christ. Art not only draws us toward the beauty of God; it gives us a heart of sympathy for other people.

12. Robert Barron, *Renewing Our Hope: Essays for the New Evangelization* (Washington, DC: The Catholic University of America Press, 2020), 283–288.

The reader may be wondering: What does all this have to do with seminary formation? Well, once again, you cannot give what you do not have! A man will only be able to draw others into this world of the spirit if he himself knows and loves and is always seeking to learn more of the beauty of the saints. The same is true of an appreciation of the authentic Catholic artistic heritage and an open but discerning approach to popular culture. He should begin cultivating these interests during his seminary years if he has not done so before. He may feel he does not have the time, but if he cannot develop his cultural interests during seminary, it's unlikely that he will find the time amidst the urgent demands of ministry. This implies that the man must take care to spend his leisure and recreation in a way that builds his soul. What music does he listen to in his free time? What podcasts? What books does he read for pleasure? What films does he watch, alone or with fellow seminarians? Are his opportunities to grow culturally stymied by too much attention to the news, whether it is politics, sports, or Hollywood gossip?

The point is ultimately not to become a walking encyclopedia of Catholic high culture but to cultivate a sense of wonder and judgment. A seminary can and should hold formal events for cultural formation, including courses in the liberal arts and voluntary film discussions. Still, it must take care to ensure that an education in beauty does not become a chore. Otherwise, this education will fail to present beauty as something that moves and attracts us. Bishop Barron recommends the great works of the Catholic heritage because he finds them fascinating, enriching, and enlivening. The disposition to allow oneself to be attracted by beauty and to share that enthusiasm and insight will be far more useful than impressive sophistication. I don't claim that early M. Night Shyamalan or

The Twilight Zone are the heights of high culture or the Catholic imagination! But they worked for me with students.

It might seem that these recommendations are a distraction from the necessary work of formation in prayer, the sacraments, ministerial skills, and theology. The priest is meant to be a mystagogue and soul doctor, after all, not a cultural connoisseur. However, just as I argued in the last chapter that there is no contradiction between Christocentrism and a serious study of classical metaphysics, so too Bishop Barron shows that Christocentrism goes hand-in-hand with a capacious approach to Catholic culture. As Barron presents them, works of art are not a distraction from Christ but rather show us his value and prepare us to understand him better. Barron writes, "The Christian tradition stubbornly and patiently walks around the icon of Christ, seeing it, describing it, speaking of it in various ways and with various audiences in mind, convinced that no one word, no one take, is sufficient to exhaust the 'infinite richness of Christ.'"[13]

And do not forget good liturgy as the height of beauty. Often, in our campus ministries, whether through an attempt to be more "youth-friendly," due to lack of a good space, or from sheer exhaustion (Holy Mass in campus ministries often begins Sunday night, as late as 10:30 p.m.!), we fail to offer a reverent Mass with a good homily and fitting (not dumbed-down) music. The Lord Jesus Christ is the All-Beautiful One, and he is fully present in the Eucharist. It is imperative that we make this reality accessible to our students through our efforts to present him in a manner worthy of his great beauty and goodness.

13. Robert Barron, *And Now I See: A Theology of Transformation* (Park Ridge, IL: Word on Fire Academic, [1998] 2021), xxvii.

LIVING THE "GOOD LIFE"

True beauty leads naturally to goodness, just as a young man in the presence of his beloved wants to dress well and stand up straight. In the course of a school year in campus ministry, this progression has a natural rhythm. September and October are good times for introductory events that highlight the beautiful, offering low barriers to entry for new students and enticing them to become more involved. As the calendar turns to November, the feasts of All Saints and All Souls are followed by readings in the liturgy concerning Christ's Second Coming. The theme of Christ's coming continues into Advent. The liturgy will thus naturally lend itself to homilies on the four last things: death, judgment, heaven, and hell. I believe that one of the biggest reasons why Christian morality has become unappealing—beige, as Bishop Barron puts it—is the loss of our "eschatological edge." People today—especially the young—have lost sight of the reality and urgency of the four last things. Of course, this can't be solved overnight: I'm not suggesting pivoting quickly from "Isn't Christian art beautiful?" to preaching fire and brimstone. But we can still ask these questions: Do we really believe that our actions and attitudes lead us toward the Lord or away from the Lord? Are we aiming for heaven or away from it? Do we know that the Lord—who is Savior and Redeemer, who is the Lord of Mercy, but also the Lord of Righteousness and the Just Judge—is coming at a time when we do not know? This should not frighten us but should make us realize that all these things—death, judgment, heaven, purgatory, and hell—are very, very real.

In other words, it's important to discuss goodness with the end in mind. In more technical terms, this is called teleology. Barron explains, "Classic moral thinkers considered the ethical act in terms of its purpose or finality."[14] The same is true not only for individual actions but for whole human lives, which is why the final measure of Christian morality is not the Ten Commandments (important as those are) but the saints. Many of the students will want to be good, but they will see morality as a box to check off through a weekend service project or a set of rules and obligations that must not be violated in a life otherwise focused on pleasure and power. None of those partial understandings are totally wrong—serving the poor is good, and there are commandments that must be obeyed—but the students will tend not to see being good as intimately tied to their happiness, to what they actually want out of life. If you start to speak to them about "the good life," they may think at first you mean "Lifestyles of the Rich and Famous,"[15] what the Italians call *la dolce vita*.

We have to contrast this secular concept of happiness with Jesus' presentation of the Beatitudes, which comes liturgically between Christmas and the beginning of Lent in two of the three cycles of readings.[16] With the help of our formation in moral philosophy and theology, particularly in the Thomistic tradition, we will need to explain to them that the good life is actually synonymous with a rich concept of happiness. The Church's rules are not a set of tripwires but a set of runway lights marking the path to taking flight, to living

14. Barron with Allen Jr., *To Light a Fire*, 75.

15. In fact, this is what I thought when I was reading a transcript for a student coming to the North American College from another Catholic institution. I added in my head, "with Robin Leach," but of course, today's college students don't know who that is! "Living the Good Life" is the name of a course about ethics and is also the name of a book about ethics; see Steven J. Jensen, *Living the Good Life: A Beginner's Thomistic Ethics* (Washington, DC: The Catholic University of America Press, 2013).

16. On the Fourth Sunday of Ordinary Time in Year A (Matthew) and the Sixth Sunday of Ordinary Time in Year B (Luke).

human life fully alive and elevated by divine grace.[17] However, the best way to initiate students into Jesus' presentation of morality and beatitude is not by instruction but by example. In this context, Barron suggests, "Show, don't tell." Allen Jr. explains:

> Barron is convinced that the moral teachings of Catholicism are true, and that people who strive to practice them will live healthier, happier, more fulfilled lives. At the same time, he knows that in a postmodern, secular world, "rule-talk" often comes off as an attempt to limit people's freedom, not to free them to become the persons God intends them to be. Therefore, the right way to deploy "the good" as a missionary tool is to start by showing people what a genuinely Christian life at its best looks like—and then, gradually, to lead people to appreciate the principles and norms which make that kind of heroic life possible.[18]

As the activities resume after Christmas break, January and early February are a time for attracting new students who didn't come in the first semester and reengaging with those who did. This would be an especially good time to bring in guest speakers or show films that highlight those living the faith in an attractive way. In my experience, personally encountering the joyfulness of religious sisters, brothers, and seminarians is the very best recruiting tool. When my own family and friends visiting me in Rome encountered the seminarians at the Pontifical North American College, they could not help but be impressed by the genuineness, faith, and generosity

17. See Irenaeus, *Against Heresies* 4.20.7.

18. Barron with Allen Jr., *To Light a Fire*, 65.

of these young men. My family and friends have told me that when they met the Religious Sisters of Mercy of Alma who bless us with their presence in that seminary, the joyfulness, intelligence, and dedication of the sisters made them want to be better Christians and better people. Encountering genuinely good and kind believers stirs up the human desire for imitation.

The coming of Lent is usually the most important time of the campus ministry year (and perhaps the parish year as well). Some students that you never otherwise see will darken your door on Ash Wednesday, and students who grew up Catholic will be habitually attuned to making sacrifices and increasing their community service during these forty days. These practices should be highly encouraged; the students are not wrong to think that these are hallmarks of the Christian life. When Jesus tells his disciples, "You are the light of the world," the backdrop is Isaiah 58, which includes a list of corporal works of mercy,[19] a list that Jesus expands in his discourse on the last judgment in Matthew 25. A transcendental approach to evangelization should not neglect goodness!

19. The liturgy for the Fifth Sunday of Ordinary Time in Year A makes this connection.

Is not this the fast that I choose:
 to loose the bonds of wickedness,
 to undo the thongs of the yoke,
to let the oppressed go free,
 and to break every yoke?
Is it not to share your bread with the hungry,
 and bring the homeless poor into your house;
when you see the naked, to cover him,
 and not to hide yourself from your own flesh?
Then shall your light break forth like the dawn,
 and your healing shall spring up speedily;
your righteousness shall go before you,
 the glory of the Lord shall be your rear guard. (Isa. 58:6–8)

However, there is a danger that can arise when campus ministries focus too much on goodness, particularly the works of mercy. Ironically, because the light of the Gospel has penetrated our culture, we can fail to distinguish ourselves from wholly secular—and often quite successful—student organizations. What makes one's service religious is that we have experienced the beguiling beauty of Christ. We can experience it in prayer (especially in the liturgy), in works of art, in creation, and even in the faces of our brothers and sisters. We love our neighbor as ourselves because we see the *imago Dei* in them, and this allows the presence of the Holy Spirit to guide and shape our encounters with the less fortunate and to see them as equals and as unique and unrepeatable persons loved by God.

I'm not suggesting that we turn students away whose first engagement with us is a service project! Rather, this perspective suggests that the campus minister should arrange for service opportunities connected to prayer or Mass and, if possible, that will put the students in contact with joyfully lived faith, such as volunteering with the Missionaries of Charity. We can focus not only on what needs to be done but also on explaining the meaning of what we are doing. For instance, the ecclesial movement Communion and Liberation has a little booklet by their founder, Luigi Giussani, called "The Meaning of Charitable Work,"[20] which could be discussed with the students, or which could serve as a model for your own simple but serious presentation of the Christian meaning of these activities.

For their own self-formation, I encourage seminarians to cultivate a greater conviction about the four last things. This does not

20. Luigi Giussani, "The Meaning of Charitable Work," Communion and Liberation website, https://english.clonline.org/cm-files/2018/05/16/file_0_1663.pdf.

happen watching (most) television! It comes by knowing the lives of the saints and especially the martyrs. The ultimate credibility of divine revelation, as Bishop Barron notes, comes in the example of the martyrs. The Roman Basilica of Santo Stefano Rotondo has some fascinating frescoes of the martyrs on the walls of the Church.[21] I urge you today to examine these paintings. They are brutal, they are grotesque, and they are disturbing, but, then again, life can be too, especially life in our contemporary world. These images are meant to shock us, to wake us up from our this-worldly slumber to the reality of what the world is for Christians—those who are in the world and yet not of the world. As Flannery O'Connor commented, "When you can assume that your audience holds the same beliefs you do, you can relax a little and use more normal ways of talking to it; when you have to assume that it does not, then you have to make your vision apparent by shock—to the hard of hearing you shout, and for the almost blind you draw large and startling figures."[22] The world, by and large, does not hold the same beliefs as the Church. It does not speak the same language as the Christian does. And this world has a deep hold on our hearts and imaginations. So the Basilica of Santo Stefano serves a powerful purpose—to shout at us Christians, urging us to wake up! The martyrs depicted here are meant to inspire courage in the hearts of Christians, imploring those with eyes to see to perceive beyond the values set by this world.

These martyrs depicted at Santo Stefano Rotondo speak to us today. These martyrs make the faith credible. They are the ultimate

21. George Weigel with Elizabeth Lev and Stephen Weigel, *Roman Pilgrimage: The Station Churches* (New York: Basic Books, 2013), 275–280.

22. Flannery O'Connor, "The Fiction Writer & His Country," in *Flannery O'Connor Collection*, ed. Matthew Becklo (Park Ridge, IL: Word on Fire Classics, 2019), 412.

expression of the credibility of divine revelation. This was true in the past and it is true in the present. To give a recent example, when ISIS savagely murdered twenty Egyptian men and a Ghanaian man on January 15, 2015, and then had the audacity to release the video a month later, stating that "Rome is next," their plan backfired. Instead of provoking fear into the hearts of the Christian world, for those who believe, these twenty Coptic Christians and one Muslim were and are inspirations. The Muslim man, Matthew Ayariga, was, by his actions, baptized in blood, convinced of the truth of the Christian faith due to the witness of his fellow workers. "Their God is my God. I will go with them," he uttered, even when he could have been pardoned by his executioners.

Our hearts, minds, and souls can thus be set ablaze for true goodness, as seen in the saints, those blessed women and men who were so in love with the Lord that they changed their lives and, in doing so, changed the world. The *Poverello* of Assisi, St. Francis, and the pugnacious "Dog of the Lord," the preacher St. Dominic, are merely two examples of the rich testimony our Church's tradition offers. The ultimate example of devotion and adherence to the one who is good, our Lord Jesus, comes in the form of the martyrs, whose witness makes credible divine revelation. They show, as Teresa of Ávila said, "Sólo Dios basta"—God alone suffices.

THE TRUTH THAT WILL SET FREE

As Lent reaches its zenith and leads to Holy Week and the Paschal Mystery, our emphasis with the students faithful to the campus ministry should become the final transcendental of truth (in Latin, *veritas*). In an age of "alternative truth," in which the very concept of objective truth is scoffed at in some circles, it can seem that truth—especially the at-times inconvenient truth of Christ calling us to repentance—could repel rather than attract. Insofar as we have the heart of a shepherd, eager to gather in the lost souls of our culture, it's understandable that we are tempted to bury the truth of the Gospel beneath reassuring platitudes. Yet it's this very tendency that has made the Church so unattractive to young people, like salt that has lost its savor (see Matt. 5:13). Barron calls this "beige" Catholicism, such as he encountered in the suburbs in the 1970s and 1980s. He explains, "It's a Catholicism that's become bland, apologetic, unsure of itself, hand-wringing, overly accommodating, that's allowed its distinctive color to blend into beige, so that it's hard to distinguish it from other religions and the wider culture."[23]

In campus ministry, catering to this approach may keep some young people from walking away—at least for a time—particularly those who have bought into various ideologies contrary to Church teaching. But if what you have to offer is no different than anything else, it will also quickly rob you of your own motivation to actually minister to them. Barron comments,

> I always go back to what John Paul said about the New Evangelization. . . . He too was worried about beige Catholicism, that we'd lost our edge, lost our fire. We had fallen into a sort of relativism, thinking that if all religions are the same, what's the point in drawing people to Jesus? Aren't we all walking up the holy mountain on different paths, and so on? I think that led to a loss of ardor, and I think that's what Ratzinger feared when he spoke of a "dictatorship of relativism." I've got my truth, you've

23. Barron with Allen Jr., *To Light a Fire*, 89.

> got your truth, and so we're all on this big lake and we're all floating along with our private opinions. I'm not going to get in your way, and you won't get in mine. You're not going to become an evangelist under those circumstances.[24]

What attracts busy students away from other possible activities is usually something vibrant, something distinctive, something with a clear and attractive quality.

Having been assured all their lives that there's no real knowledge and no real truth in religious matters, those who are drawn into your teaching and preaching often develop an intense hunger to know, to learn as much as possible. The key to getting them there is an approach that Word on Fire calls "affirmative orthodoxy." On his podcast, Barron explains, "Affirmative orthodoxy means no compromising when it comes to the great teachings of the Church, either doctrinally or morally. But it's expressed in a positive, affirming way rather than a negative and finger-wagging way. That's the trick now with evangelization. We don't start with 'Don't do this' and 'The culture's wrong over there.' We begin with the beauty and the integrity of the Christian thing."[25]

Cardinal Timothy Dolan of New York echoes Barron on this point: "The Catholic Church affirms, strengthens, expands what's most noble, most beautiful, most sacred, in the human project. I like to quote a line from Father Robert Barron, that the Church only says no to another no, and two nos make a yes. It's only when

24. Barron with Allen Jr., 109–110.

25. "102: Affirmative Orthodoxy," *Word on Fire Show* podcast, November 20, 2017, https://www.wordonfire.org/videos/wordonfire-show/episode102/.

the yes of humanity is threatened that the Church will say no, to protect the yes."[26]

The Church is a yes, always a yes, to everyone and everything that is good and holy and pure (or is at least striving to become so). Bishop Barron recognizes this, and that is why he is open to dialogue even with those who may at first seem to be on "the other side." We can see this in his interviews with figures like Dr. Jordan Peterson and Ben Shapiro, as well as in his talks at Google and his AMAs ("Ask Me Anything") on Reddit.

However far students may be from true, orthodox Christian practice and belief when they come to the campus ministry, we have to look for as much as possible that we can say yes to and encourage. If any of the increasing numbers of atheists and agnostics come to confront us, we can at least acknowledge that we agree that "something important is at stake."[27] Many of those who come to participate without argument will not be truly orthodox believers but will be imbued with what Notre Dame sociologist Christian Smith calls "moral therapeutic deism." He and Melinda Lundquist Denton, in their 2005 work *Soul Searching: The Religious and Spiritual Lives of American Teenagers*,[28] described its contours as loosely consisting in the following, related tenets:

1. A God exists who created and ordered the world and watches over human life on earth.

26. Timothy Dolan with John L. Allen Jr., *A People of Hope: Archbishop Timothy Dolan in Conversation* (New York: Image Books, 2012).

27. Robert Barron, *Centered: The Spirituality of Word on Fire* (Park Ridge, IL: Word on Fire, 2020), 110.

28. Christian Smith with Melinda Lundquist Denton, *Soul Searching: The Religious and Spiritual Lives of American Teenagers* (Oxford: Oxford University Press, 2005).

2. God wants people to be good, nice and fair to each other, as taught in the Bible and by most world religions.

3. The central goal of life is to be happy and to feel good about oneself.

4. God does not need to be particularly involved in one's life except when God is needed to resolve a problem.

5. Good people go to heaven when they die.[29]

Moral therapeutic deism is a kind of residue of Christian teaching. Compared to the full truth of the Gospel, it's pretty thin, and it's likely that the students who believe it do so without much conviction. But then again, there are true or at least partially true beliefs in that list that can be the starting point for a greater conversion.

The notion of God as Creator can be drawn into a discussion about how grand such a Creator must be and why we not only acknowledge him but worship him. Jesus certainly did teach the Golden Rule, but his challenges regarding anger, lust, and the love of one's enemies can provoke more serious discussion about what kindness and hospitality really mean and how the claim of Jesus to be God allows him to set a higher standard. The theme of true happiness can be a hook for an invitation to study great philosophy like Aristotle, great theology like St. Thomas, or great apologetics like G.K. Chesterton.[30] Most campus ministries attempt nothing so intel-

29. Smith with Denton, 162–163.

30. Barron names Chesterton and Thomas Aquinas as paragons of affirmative orthodoxy in *Centered*, 111.

lectually ambitious as reading St. Thomas with their students—and sometimes that is prudent given the student population. The point is to challenge students at the ministry on the same intellectual level that they are getting from their regular classes. If you're at a campus full of first-generation college students struggling to pass their courses, the last thing you want to do is to make the campus ministry another intellectual struggle. On the other hand, if you're ministering to Ivy League students, you had better be ready for an intellectual struggle yourself! In any setting, study of the Bible is an attractive and powerful way to bring students into contact with the truths of the faith. To quote a saying that is often attributed to St. Jerome, "The Scriptures are shallow enough for a babe to come and drink without fear of drowning and deep enough for a theologian to swim in without ever touching the bottom."

The real problem with moral therapeutic deism—and therefore the real opportunity for the evangelist—is the "deism" itself, point four on the list. We have to show students that God desires to enter into intimacy with them, communion with them—that God has called us beyond our natural capacities to live a truly divine life. The scandal of bad actors in the Church—and the scandal of the (hopefully venial) sins the students see in you—will push you to give a truly nuanced approach to what is divine and what is human in the Christian life. Over time, as they pray and follow your example, students will be more open to seeing the splendor of God's self-revelation and contemplate even more lofty mysteries such as the Incarnation of the Son of God or the eternal procession of the Trinity. It is essential, in any case, to try to get the students not only participating in the ministry but also reading Catholic works. Their time with you may be as much as four years or it may be less than one. For them to carry what they've experienced and learned on to their future destinations, the best companions are the great works of Catholic thinking to which you've introduced them.[31]

For the seminarian himself, the primary task of self-formation in the truth is just to do his studies (see chapter 6). However, I also encourage the men to take as their models and guides thinkers like Thomas, Chesterton, and Barron, who practice this way of thinking. It's too easy to take in all of the theological information presented in seminary but to make one's real judgments based on excessively negative Catholic voices (particularly on internet sites) who rant about the state of the culture, about the state of the Church and ecclesial politics, and about the dangers of modernism or other forms of heresy, real or imagined. I don't say that we should be naïve about evil in the Church or the world! Jesus certainly wasn't, and neither was Paul. Nevertheless, a focus on the truth in isolation from beauty and goodness can lead us to be rigid and bitter, the exact opposite of who Christ calls us to become as shepherds. It will come across as inauthentic to pursue affirmative orthodoxy with one's students when one's heart is fixed on condemnation after hours, in conversation with friends, or in time spent online. I recommend especially the writings of Pope Benedict XVI as exemplary of someone who was an incisive critic of all that was wrong and yet a tireless practitioner of affirmative orthodoxy.

CONCLUSION

I have focused in this chapter on campus ministry as one potential pastoral situation that gels nicely with Barron's approach to

31. Or at the very least, get them listening to Catholic podcasts with solid intellectual content.

evangelization through the transcendentals. I do think that some of these lessons will apply as well in other ministry settings, including the parish. In any parish in which there is a healthy number of families with children, the same school-year dynamic is at play, with September/October being prime recruiting time, and Lent being the portion of the year in which the most intense activity occurs. The focus on the last things in November and December and the climax of the year in the Triduum and the Easter Season are simply dimensions of the liturgical year.

The biggest difference between the campus ministry setting and the parish setting is that in a campus ministry, there is much more turnover and a greater sense of energy and drive. Students are, like the campus minister himself, temporary guests at the college or university, destined to depart after four years (or in the case of a study abroad program, one year). By contrast, most parishes have long-term members who have been there before the priest and will likely be there long afterward. This makes the task both easier and harder: there is a longer period over which to practice mystagogy and soul doctoring, but there is also likely to be more resistance to any kind of change.

It's easy to become frustrated by such institutional inertia, but that would be a mistake. If we can follow Barron in affirming whatever is beautiful, good, and true in confused college students or even atheists, we should certainly do the same toward the existing practices we find in our parish assignment. Tend and encourage the positive and slowly diminish and weed out the negative; even if your heart burns (as mine does) to make the liturgy as beautiful as possible, it may take time and patience to acclimate the parish to a higher vision of worship. Be "not self-centered, aloof, judgmental, or self-imposing but instead . . . characterized by a 'serene openness' and capable of listening and collaboration."[32]

Similarly, it takes time to shift a parish out of the mode of maintenance and into a mode of evangelizing the surrounding area through beauty, goodness, and truth. The first task, actually, is to follow Jesus' example and work on evangelizing a smaller number of "disciples" of your own—the members of the parish staff, the leaders of various ministries, and the most active families. However dedicated they may be to Jesus and to the parish, they may be so focused on their existing understanding of either goodness or truth that they would actually be resistant to a fresh approach to living and sharing the faith. They may think they know better than you, especially when you are early in your priesthood and they have decades of experience. Here, just as with agnostic college students, it seems reasonable to me to follow the *via pulchritudinis*—to lure them with beauty into a deeper relationship with the Mystery and a deeper healing through Christ's Sacred Heart. How surprising they may find a film like *Babette's Feast*,[33] for instance, and how surprised they may be to find in you a priest not simply punching the clock and dispensing the sacraments, but one who has a genuine heart for beauty, who sees goodness as intimately related to their desire for happiness, and who sees the truth as liberating. Once they see that their pastor's humanity is fully alive, they may become more open to following him in the truly divine work of evangelization.

And no priest can hope to evangelize alone. Even an internet evangelist like Robert Barron would never be able to reach his

32. *Program of Priestly Formation* 367.

33. Barron, *Renewing Our Hope*, 272–277.

audience without his team at Word on Fire. Evangelization on the ground—even more than through media—requires individual, personal attention to every man, woman, and child of Christ's flock. No priest has enough time for everyone, even in a small parish. Rather, having been formed humanly, spiritually, intellectually, and pastorally, he needs to lead the ongoing formation of his ministry team and the families of his parish.[34]

The ministry of a priest is not to replace the work of his deacons and lay collaborators but to make it possible through the sacraments and to enhance it. As he is particularly conformed to Christ as priest, prophet, and king, so must the priest make his parishioners more aware of their baptismal call into the same three offices. As he is in love with Christ's Bride, despite the flaws and sins of her members, so must the priest enliven in his parishioners the same deep metaphysical understanding of the Church as one, holy, catholic, and apostolic that can ground all of their practical efforts. As he is a mystagogue, leading others into the mysteries of God, the priest must equip a team of catechists and evangelizers who are themselves in dialogue with the Mystery. As he is a soul doctor, the priest must build a "medical team" attentive to the spiritual ills of parishioners and a parish culture that encourages spiritual health and growth. He must help his parish—but especially his collaborators in ministry—to grow in the dimensions of human formation, spiritual formation, intellectual formation, and pastoral formation according to the same principles that he himself imbibed in the seminary. He must "show" and not just "tell" by remaining faithful to prayer,

34. One resource that some parishes have found helpful is Sherry Waddell, *Forming Intentional Disciples* (Huntington, IN: Our Sunday Visitor, 2012) and her Catherine of Siena Institute. But there are many others.

exercise, and a healthy diet and seeking experience of the beautiful, good, and true. The priest must cut back on other work, delegate tasks, and resist becoming a "hyphenated priest."

In the end, this is my advice to priests. Know the Lord, let him give you your identity, and do all that you do out of who you are: a priest of Jesus Christ. And remain faithful to study. Never become the priest without books! Never become the priest who collects books and doesn't crack them open. I am grateful for everyone who has read this book—priests, men discerning, and the faithful interested in the role of the priest—and I hope that through the theology of Robert Barron, you have a renewed appreciation for the Catholic priesthood in all its dimensions. But don't stop here! Read Barron's books. Read Thomas Aquinas. Learn about God and bring that learning into your relationship with God.

Then we will truly set the world ablaze. And then may the Lord ask you what you truly desire, and may you respond with sincerity, "Nothing but you, Lord."

Conclusion

As we conclude this text, we should never forget that there are four dimensions of priestly formation, all of them building on one another. Like the legs of a chair, take one out and it collapses. Like the legs of a chair, elongate one and you have an imbalance.

The *human* dimension of formation, making sure that the man is psychologically and physically healthy, as well as affectively mature, is the basis on which to build.

The *spiritual* dimension of formation, as we have seen indicated in Bishop Barron's work, is the *sine qua non*; unless the man has a true and deep relationship in prayer to Christ in his Church, then he cannot serve the people of God, for *nemo dat quod non habet* (you can't give what you don't have).

The *intellectual* dimension of formation is essential. He cannot communicate the truths of the faith if he does not know them. The seminarian must sacrifice himself on the altar of his desk, knowing, with the same professional rigor of a doctor, the truths of the faith from his study of orthodox Catholic theology. His studies must have the structure of a solid philosophical background and come from a true immersion in the Catholic imagination, which includes art, history, literature, and many other fields in the liberal arts.[1]

The *pastoral* dimension of formation is where the "rubber hits the road," where the seminarian puts into practice what he has been given in the other pillars of formation. It is in this pastoral pillar of formation that the seminarian, the future priest, can exhibit his understanding of being a "mystagogue" and a "soul-doctor."

A young Fr. Barron, when asked if his vision of a heroic priesthood, a priest who is a doctor of the soul and a mystagogue, would be successful in parochial ministry, replied,

> I do believe that priests no longer see the parish as a glamorous, exciting place to practice their craft, and that's a shame. Fifty years ago, the great priests of Chicago, for example, were very parish-focused; they saw the parish as an interesting place where they could live out their love of the mind and the spirit. The parish was a testing ground for all the great stuff they had learned in the seminary. My fear is that the parish has become flattened out, banalized.
>
> If I can use the doctor analogy again, I want doctors of the soul who are not going to stay in the lab and do more research, but who are going to hit the road with new medicines. If the parish is seen as a place of drudgery, or simply a local branch of the general store, then it loses its poetry. When we lose our poetry, we lose our soul. Today we call the priest the "presider

1. Saint Phillip's Seminary at the Oratory in Toronto offers a fascinating "Map Year" in which a seminarian learns to immerse himself in the classics of Western civilization (https://oratory-toronto.org/map-year/).

at liturgy," or the "president of the assembly." Give me a break. It sounds like a Boy Scout leader.

French theologian Jesuit Father Pierre Teilhard de Chardin said the priest calls down fire on the earth. Now we're talking! If you're a young eighteen-year-old, why would you want to be the president of the assembly? When I was in the seminary, they used to say the priest was the "organizer of ministries." Sure, that's a part of priesthood. But who's going to be lit on fire by a term like that?

How about, "You're the one that calls down fire on the earth." Or as James Joyce said, you're a "priest of the beautiful." You're a bearer of the power of God, which is the beautiful itself. You're an artist. You're a poet, a shaman, a mystic. Those terms will light up a few souls.[2]

Bishop Barron as a theologian has truly contributed to the theology of the priesthood. I know that his images of the priesthood have helped me in my own daily living out of the priesthood. For him, the priest is the mystagogue, the soul doctor, the man of the sacraments, the one who calls fire down on earth. What better image can we have for the priest today?

2. "How to Build a Better Priest: The Editors Interview Father Robert Barron," *U.S. Catholic* 62, no. 12 (December 1997): 14.